DIABETIC AIR FRYER
COOKBOOK FOR BEGINNERS

Healthy and Easy Low-Carb, Low-Fat, Low-Sugar & Vegetarian Diabetic Air Fryer Recipes

VICTORIA STONE

TABLE OF CONTENTS

INTRODUCTION

Welcome to the Diabetic Air Fryer Cookbook, a culinary adventure that fuses the cutting-edge technique of air frying with the tenets of diabetic-friendly eating. In this introduction, we will look at the many advantages of utilizing an air fryer as a useful tool for making tasty, nutritious meals that are specifically designed for people with diabetes.

Diabetes is a metabolic disease that is defined by high blood sugar levels that are brought on by the incapacity of the body to make or use insulin efficiently. The hormone insulin helps blood sugar enter cells more easily so that it may be used as fuel. When this mechanism is interfered with, blood sugar levels must be stabilized through careful dietary planning.

A healthy diet is essential for effectively treating diabetes. Maintaining blood sugar within a healthy range requires careful consideration of the kinds and amounts of lipids, proteins, carbohydrates, and total calories consumed. Not only is regulating blood sugar levels a priority, but heart health promotion, weight control, and averting complications from diabetes are also.

Each recipe in this cookbook has been thoughtfully created to satisfy the dietary requirements of those who have diabetes. Whole, nutrient-dense foods and thoughtful cooking methods are our top priorities when preparing tasty meals that follow nutritional recommendations for managing diabetes.

You will discover a variety of dishes, ranging from delectable appetizers to enticing sweets, all customized for the air fryer and fit for a diabetic-friendly way of life.

General Guide when Choosing Food to Eat

When you're managing your diet, especially with diabetes, it's important not to cut out any whole category of food. Although it's wise to eat less starch and sugar if you have diabetes, your body still needs carbohydrates. So, the key is not to eliminate carbs completely but to make smart choices. Pick the healthiest options within each food group, avoiding those that could spike your blood sugar or harm your health.

The main aim when you have diabetes is to choose foods that don't cause your blood sugar to rise excessively. You should eat foods that keep you satisfied and curb hunger. Also, some foods can boost your overall health and provide nutrients that help combat diabetes and its side effects.

Foods Low in Starch

Opt for whole grains like oatmeal, quinoa, and brown rice instead of white rice, white flour, or heavily processed grains such as macaroni. Choose baked sweet potatoes over high-carb alternatives like French fries. Steer clear of white bread and similar items rich in white flour. Instead, select whole grain products that are free from or have minimal added sugars.

Vegetables Low in Starch

Incorporating several servings of non-starchy vegetables daily is a great strategy for anyone with diabetes. These veggies are so low in calories that it's hard to overeat them. Aim for at least five servings of fruits and vegetables each day, with a minimum of three servings from the non-starchy category.

Here are some examples:

- *Leafy greens include kale, lettuce, spinach, watercress, cabbage, and Brussels sprouts.*

- *Root vegetables like carrots, turnips, and radishes.*

- *Gourds and squashes such as cucumber, squash, zoodles (zucchini noodles), and pumpkin.*

- *Stalky veggies like asparagus, leeks, spring onions, and celery.*

- *Other beneficial choices are broccoli, bean sprouts, mushrooms, cauliflower, peppers, and tomatoes.*

Vegetables are indeed a powerful ally in managing diabetes. Consuming them fresh, whether raw or gently cooked (steamed, roasted, grilled), offers a wealth of health benefits and keeps carbs in check. Even frozen veggies that are lightly steamed are a good pick.

Choose canned vegetables with no added salt or those labeled low in sodium to avoid unnecessary salt intake.

Fatty Fish

Examples include herring, salmon, anchovies, mackerel, and sardines. Fatty fish are consistently recommended in diets aimed at preventing various health issues, and managing diabetes is one of those instances. They're incredibly beneficial for those with diabetes, offering a rich source of omega-3 fatty acids which are crucial for heart health.

Dairy Products

Dairy items such as milk, yogurt, cream, butter, and cheese, especially when unsweetened, can be excellent for a low-carb diet. They provide valuable nutrients like protein, calcium, and vitamin B12. The National Osteoporosis Society suggests adults need around 0,7 g of calcium daily for bone health and other bodily functions reliant on calcium.

When it comes to dairy, choosing low-fat options is generally advisable if you're watching your fat intake. However, you can still enjoy full-fat dairy in moderation. Healthier dairy choices include skim milk, low-fat yogurt, and low-fat or non-fat sour cream or cottage cheese. On the other hand, it's best to limit intake of whole milk, regular yogurt, standard sour cream, regular cottage cheese, and ice cream.

Beans and Legumes

Beans and legumes like lentils, peas, chickpeas, and runner beans are excellent plant-based protein sources that can greatly benefit individuals with diabetes. Among these, soya beans stand out, with studies showing they can enhance insulin sensitivity and lower the risk of type 2 diabetes development. In some Asian countries, black soya beans are specifically utilized to manage type 2 diabetes. Incorporating beans into your salads is an effective way to boost your protein intake without adding many calories.

Lean Meat

Lean meats are proteins that are low in fat and calories, such as pork chops with fat trimmed off, or skinless poultry like chicken or turkey. They're not just a vital source of protein aiding in cellular repair and growth but also offer low carb and low-fat options. Poultry is especially rich in B vitamins, choline, and selenium. Vitamin B3, or niacin, found in these meats, assists in managing stress and sexual hormones—key for those with diabetes who may face related health issues. It also supports nerve function and reduces inflammation. Selenium, known for its antioxidant properties, aids in controlling inflammation and cellular protection, while also supporting the immune system, crucial for individuals with diabetes.

Eggs

When it comes to eggs, it's essential to monitor your intake due to their potential impact on cholesterol levels. Boiled eggs are recommended to be consumed whole to leverage all their nutrients, not just the whites. While eggs are low in carbs and rich in vital nutrients like essential fatty acids and vitamin D, excessive consumption could pose risks due to their cholesterol content. Therefore, while eggs offer significant nutritional benefits, they should be consumed in moderation, particularly by individuals managing diabetes.

Nuts

Cashews: Including cashews in your diet can help lower blood pressure and reduce the risk of heart disease, which in turn can decrease the likelihood of developing type 2 diabetes. They are low in calories and fat, making them a good choice for not impacting your blood sugar or weight negatively. A daily handful of cashews is recommended for optimal benefits.

PEANUTS: High in fiber and protein, peanuts are an excellent snack for those with diabetes. They can be enjoyed in moderation—about 25 to 30 nuts per day—and roasting them is a tasty option. Peanuts can help manage blood sugar levels effectively.

PISTACHIOS: While pistachios are energy-dense, they are beneficial due to their protein and healthy fat content, which can help you feel satiated and reduce snacking urges. Research indicates that pistachios can be particularly advantageous for individuals with diabetes. Choose unsalted pistachios to avoid excess sodium.

WALNUTS: Despite their high calorie content, walnuts don't negatively influence body weight and offer numerous nutritional benefits. Consuming them regularly can support weight management, activate fat-burning processes, and reduce fasting glucose levels, helping to prevent obesity related to diabetes. Their energy content also helps curb excessive eating.

ALMONDS: Almonds aid in regulating blood sugar levels and are especially beneficial for reducing the oxidative stress that impacts individuals with diabetes. They are also a good magnesium source. For a healthier option, avoid salted almonds and consider soaking them overnight to consume the next day.

FOODS TO AVOID

Sugar-Sweetened Beverages

Drinks sweetened with sugar are particularly bad for diabetics due to their high carbohydrate content. For instance, a 12 oz can of soda contains about 38 grams of carbs, similar to sweetened iced teas and lemonades, which have around 35 grams of carbs per serving. Additionally, these beverages are loaded with fructose, which is linked to increased insulin resistance and exacerbation of diabetes. High fructose intake can lead to abdominal fat accumulation, harmful cholesterol increases, and higher triglyceride levels, complicating diabetes management and metabolic health.

Trans Fats

Trans fats are created by hydrogenating unsaturated fats to make them more stable. You can find them in products like margarine and some frozen meals, and they are often added to muffins and baked goods to enhance flavour and shelf life. While trans fats don't directly raise blood sugar levels, they contribute to insulin resistance and fat accumulation, disrupting fat metabolism and lowering beneficial cholesterol levels. This can indirectly impair diabetes control. Moreover, since people with diabetes have a higher risk of heart disease, consuming trans fats exacerbates this risk, further emphasizing the importance of avoiding these fats for overall health and diabetes management.

Pasta, Rice, and White Bread

These staples are high in carbohydrates and break down quickly, leading to rapid spikes in blood glucose levels. Research indicates that consuming high-carb foods like bagels can significantly increase blood sugar levels and impair cognitive function in individuals with type 2 diabetes. Moreover, such foods offer little nutritional value and are deficient in fiber, which is crucial for managing diabetes, cholesterol, and blood pressure. A diet rich in fiber is essential for good health, particularly for those managing diabetes, hence the emphasis should be on high-fiber foods.

Fruit-Flavored Yogurt

While plain yogurt can be a nutritious choice for those with diabetes, fruit-flavoured varieties tell a different story. These products, often made from non-fat or low-fat milk, are packed with added sugars and carbohydrates. For example, a single serving of fruit-flavoured yogurt can contain around 47 grams of sugar, primarily in the form of added sugars. To support gut health, weight management, and blood sugar control, it's better to choose plain, whole-milk yogurt without added sugars.

Regarding fruits, it's also wise for diabetics to be mindful of their choices and consumption levels, focusing on those with lower sugar content and monitoring portion sizes to prevent blood sugar spikes.

GRAPES: Each grape has about 1 gram of carbohydrates, so eating 2 grapes translates to consuming 2 grams of carbs. In comparison, you could eat a similar quantity of berries or strawberries and ingest far fewer carbohydrates, making these a better choice for managing blood sugar levels.

CHERRIES: Although delicious, cherries are high in sugar, making it easy to overconsume and experience rapid increases in blood sugar. Enjoying cherries in moderation is key to preventing spikes in glucose levels.

PINEAPPLE: This fruit has a high glycemic index when ripe, which can lead to quick rises in blood sugar. If you choose to eat pineapple, limit yourself to a small portion, such as half a cup, and pair it with a low-fat food like Greek yogurt to balance the meal. Avoid canned pineapple, as it is typically laden with added sugars.

MANGO: Despite their delightful taste, mangos are high in carbohydrates and sugars, with a single mango containing around 2 grams of carbs. The glycemic index of a mango increases as it ripens, so a firmer mango will have a slightly lower index. However, moderation is still essential.

BANANA: Known for their sweetness, bananas are carbohydrate-dense, with a medium banana containing twice as many carbs as many other fruits. If you're craving a banana, consider eating only half and storing the rest for later.

DRIED FRUITS: While they may seem like a convenient snack, dried fruits like raisins are concentrated sources of sugar and carbohydrates. Just two tablespoons of raisins can have as many carbs as a cup of whole fruits like blueberries. Opting for fresh fruits over dried ones is a healthier choice to avoid excessive sugar and carb intake.

BREAKFAST

CRISPY CAULIFLOWER BREAKFAST HASH

INGREDIENTS

- *400g cauliflower florets*
- *100g cherry tomatoes, halved*
- *1 small onion, diced*
- *2 cloves garlic, minced*
- *30ml olive oil*
- *1 tsp paprika*
- *1/2 tsp dried thyme*
- *Salt and pepper to taste*
- *2 eggs*
- *Fresh parsley for garnish (optional)*

Cal 220 | Fat 14 g | Carb 18 g | Protein 8 g | Serving 2 | Cook time 20 min

INSTRUCTIONS

1. Preheat the air fryer to 200°C in the roast mode.
2. In a large bowl, toss cauliflower florets, cherry tomatoes, diced onion, minced garlic, olive oil, paprika, thyme, salt, and pepper until evenly coated.
3. Spread the mixture evenly in the air fryer basket.
4. Cook for 15-20 minutes, shaking the basket halfway through, until cauliflower is crispy and golden brown.
5. Meanwhile, fry eggs in a non-stick pan until desired doneness.
6. Serve the crispy cauliflower hash topped with fried eggs.
7. Garnish with fresh parsley if desired.

Veggie Omelette

INSTRUCTIONS

1. Preheat your air fryer to 180°C using the Air Fry mode.
2. In a bowl, whisk the eggs with a pinch of salt and pepper.
3. Heat olive oil in a non-stick pan over medium heat. Sauté the onion and red Sweet Pepper until softened.
4. Add cherry tomatoes and spinach to the pan. Cook until spinach wilts.
5. Pour the whisked eggs over the vegetables in the pan. Swirl the pan to distribute evenly.
6. Cook until the edges of the omelette start to set, then sprinkle grated cheese on one half.
7. Fold the omelette in half and transfer it to the air fryer basket.
8. Air fry for 5-7 minutes or until the omelette is cooked through and slightly golden.
9. Serve hot with a side of whole grain toast if desired.

INGREDIENTS

* 4 large eggs
* 50g cherry tomatoes, halved
* 50g baby spinach leaves
* 30g red Sweet Pepper, diced
* 30g onion, finely chopped
* Salt and pepper to taste
* 5ml olive oil
* 10g low-fat cheddar cheese, grated

Cal 190 | Fat 13 g | Carb 5 g | Protein 14 g | Serving 2 | Cook time 15 min

Savory Spinach and Feta Breakfast Muffins

INGREDIENTS

* 150g fresh spinach, chopped
* 100g feta cheese, crumbled
* 1 small onion, finely diced
* 2 cloves garlic, minced
* 4 eggs
* 50ml milk
* 30ml olive oil
* 100g almond flour
* 1 g baking powder
* Salt and pepper to taste

Cal 180 | Fat 11 g | Carb 12 g | Protein 7 g | Serving 2 | Cook time 18 min

INSTRUCTIONS

1. Preheat the air fryer to 180°C in the bake mode.
2. In a skillet, heat olive oil over medium heat. Add diced onion and minced garlic, and cook until softened, about 5 minutes. Add chopped spinach and cook until wilted. Remove from heat and let cool.
3. In a large bowl, whisk together eggs and milk. Stir in cooled spinach mixture.
4. Add crumbled feta cheese, almond flour, baking powder, salt, and pepper to the bowl. Mix until well combined.
5. Divide the batter evenly among greased muffin cups.
6. Place the muffin tray in the air fryer basket.
7. Bake for 15-18 minutes until muffins are golden brown and cooked through.
8. Let cool for a few minutes before serving.

Spiced Chickpea Breakfast Bowl

INSTRUCTIONS

1. Preheat the air fryer to 200°C in the roast mode.
2. In a bowl, toss chickpeas with olive oil, ground cumin, paprika, salt, and pepper until evenly coated.
3. Spread the seasoned chickpeas on the air fryer tray in a single layer.
4. Roast for 10-12 minutes until chickpeas are crispy and golden brown.
5. Meanwhile, fry eggs in a non-stick pan until desired doneness.
6. In serving bowls, layer baby spinach leaves, roasted chickpeas, cherry tomatoes, diced avocado, and fried eggs.
7. Garnish with fresh cilantro if desired.
8. Serve hot.

INGREDIENTS

* *200g canned chickpeas, drained and rinsed*
* *100g cherry tomatoes, halved*
* *50g baby spinach leaves*
* *1 small avocado, diced*
* *2 eggs*
* *15ml olive oil*
* *1 tsp ground cumin*
* *1/2 tsp paprika*
* *Salt and pepper to taste*
* *Fresh coriander for garnish (optional)*

Cal 180 | Fat 11 g | Carb 12 g | Protein 6 g | Serving 2 | Cook time 18 min

MEDITERRANEAN AUBERGINE AND TOMATO BREAKFAST BAKE

INGREDIENTS

* *1 large aubergine, diced*
* *200g cherry tomatoes, halved*
* *1 small red onion, sliced*
* *2 cloves garlic, minced*
* *30ml olive oil*
* *1 tsp dried oregano*
* *1/2 tsp smoked paprika*
* *Salt and pepper to taste*
* *4 eggs*
* *Fresh basil leaves for garnish (optional)*

Cal 220 | Fat 16 g | Carb 12 g | Protein 9 g | Serving 2 | Cook time 30 min

INSTRUCTIONS

1. Preheat the air fryer to 180°C in the bake mode.
2. In a large bowl, toss diced aubergine, cherry tomatoes, sliced red onion, minced garlic, olive oil, dried oregano, smoked paprika, salt, and pepper until well coated.
3. Spread the mixture evenly in the air fryer basket.
4. Bake for 20-25 minutes, stirring halfway through, until the vegetables are tender and slightly caramelized.
5. Create four wells in the cooked vegetable mixture and crack an egg into each well.
6. Return the basket to the air fryer and bake for an additional 5-7 minutes, or until the egg whites are set but the yolks are still runny.
7. Garnish with fresh basil leaves before serving, if desired.
8. Serve hot.

CRUNCHY COCONUT-CRUSTED FRENCH TOAST STICKS

INSTRUCTIONS

1. Preheat the air fryer to 180°C in the bake mode.
2. Cut each slice of bread into strips to form sticks.
3. In a shallow bowl, whisk together eggs, coconut milk, ground cinnamon, and vanilla extract.
4. In another shallow bowl, spread shredded coconut.
5. Dip each bread stick into the egg mixture, allowing excess to drip off, then coat it with shredded coconut.
6. Place the coated sticks on a baking sheet lined with parchment paper.
7. Lightly spray the sticks with olive oil spray.
8. Arrange the sticks in the air fryer basket in a single layer, making sure they are not touching.
9. Bake for 8-10 minutes, flipping halfway through, until golden and crispy.
10. Serve warm with maple syrup or your favourite dipping sauce.

INGREDIENTS

* 4 slices wholemeal bread
* 2 eggs
* 60ml unsweetened coconut milk
* 30g shredded coconut
* 1/2 tsp ground cinnamon
* 1.25ml vanilla extract
* Olive oil spray

Cal 180 | Fat 7 g | Carb 15 g | Protein 7 g | Serving 2 | Cook time 15 min

Cheesy Broccoli and Mushroom Breakfast Frittata

INGREDIENTS

- 100g broccoli florets, chopped
- 100g mushrooms, sliced
- 1 small onion, diced
- 4 eggs
- 50ml milk
- 50g grated cheddar cheese
- 15ml olive oil
- Salt and pepper to taste

Cal 250 | Fat 18 g | Carb 8 g | Protein 15 g | Serving 2 | Cook time 20 min

INSTRUCTIONS

1. Preheat the air fryer to 180°C in the bake mode.
2. In a non-stick skillet, heat olive oil over medium heat. Add diced onion and cook until softened, about 3-4 minutes.
3. Add chopped broccoli florets and sliced mushrooms to the skillet. Cook until vegetables are tender, about 5 minutes.
4. In a bowl, whisk together eggs, milk, grated cheddar cheese, salt, and pepper.
5. Pour the egg mixture over the cooked vegetables in the skillet. Stir gently to distribute the vegetables evenly.
6. Transfer the mixture to an air fryer-safe dish.
7. Bake in the air fryer for 12-15 minutes until the frittata is set and the top is golden brown.
8. Allow to cool slightly before slicing and serving.

CRISP EGG CUPS

INSTRUCTIONS

1. Preheat the air fryer to 180°C in the bake mode.
2. Grease four wells of a muffin tin with olive oil spray.
3. Crack one egg into each muffin well.
4. Divide chopped spinach and halved cherry tomatoes evenly among the egg-filled wells.
5. Season with salt and pepper to taste.
6. Sprinkle grated Parmesan cheese over the top of each egg cup.
7. Place the muffin tin in the air fryer basket.
8. Bake for 10-12 minutes until the egg whites are set and the yolks are still slightly runny.
9. Remove from the air fryer and let cool for a few minutes before serving.
10. Carefully remove the egg cups from the muffin tin and serve hot.

INGREDIENTS

* 4 large eggs
* 50g spinach, chopped
* 50g cherry tomatoes, halved
* 30g grated Parmesan cheese
* Salt and pepper to taste
* Olive oil spray

Cal 90 | Fat 6 g | Carb 2 g | Protein 8 g | Serving 2 | Cook time 12 min

AIR FRYER BREAKFAST PIZZA

INGREDIENTS

* *1 whole wheat pita bread or flatbread*
* *2 tbsp tomato sauce*
* *50g shredded mozzarella cheese*
* *2 slices turkey bacon, cooked and crumbled*
* *1 egg*
* *1/4 red sweet pepper, diced*
* *Salt and pepper to taste*
* *Olive oil spray*

Cal 350 | Fat 15 g | Carb 12 g | Protein 20 g | Serving 2 | Cook time 15 min

INSTRUCTIONS

1. Preheat the air fryer to 180°C in the bake mode.
2. Place the pita bread or flatbread on a flat surface.
3. Spread tomato sauce evenly over the surface of the bread.
4. Sprinkle shredded mozzarella cheese on top of the sauce.
5. Scatter cooked and crumbled turkey bacon and diced red sweet pepper over the cheese.
6. Create a small well in the centre of the pizza and crack an egg into it.
7. Season with salt and pepper to taste.
8. Lightly spray the air fryer basket with olive oil spray.
9. Carefully transfer the pizza to the air fryer basket.
10. Bake for 8-10 minutes until the egg is cooked to your desired doneness and the cheese is melted and bubbly.
11. Remove from the air fryer and let cool for a few minutes before slicing and serving.

EGG AND AVOCADO TOAST

INSTRUCTIONS

1. Preheat the air fryer to 180°C in the toast mode.
2. While the air fryer is preheating, halve the avocado, remove the pit, and scoop the flesh into a bowl. Mash the avocado with a fork until smooth.
3. Lightly toast the slices of whole wheat bread in the air fryer for 2-3 minutes.
4. Once toasted, spread the mashed avocado evenly on each slice of toast.
5. Carefully crack one egg onto each slice of toast, making sure to keep the yolks intact.
6. Season with salt and pepper to taste.
7. Place the thinly sliced red sweet pepper on top of the avocado.
8. Lightly spray the air fryer basket with olive oil spray.
9. Place the avocado toast with eggs in the air fryer basket.
10. Air fry for 5-6 minutes, or until the egg whites are set and the yolks are cooked to your desired level of doneness.
11. Remove from the air fryer and serve with a dollop of cottage cheese on top of each toast.

INGREDIENTS

* 2 slices whole wheat bread
* 1 ripe avocado
* 2 eggs
* 1/4 red sweet pepper, thinly sliced
* 50g cottage cheese
* Salt and pepper to taste
* Olive oil spray

Cal 250 | Fat 15 g | Carb 17 g | Protein 14 g | Serving 2 | Cook time 15 min

LUNCH

MEDITERRANEAN STUFFED SWEET PEPPERS

INSTRUCTIONS

1. Preheat the air fryer to 180°C in the bake mode.
2. In a skillet over medium heat, cook the ground turkey or chicken until browned and cooked through. Remove from the skillet and set aside.
3. In the same skillet, add a little olive oil if needed and sauté the chopped onion and minced garlic until softened.
4. In a large bowl, combine the cooked ground meat, sautéed onion and garlic, cooked quinoa, diced cherry tomatoes, crumbled feta cheese, chopped fresh parsley, dried oregano, salt, and pepper. Mix until well combined.
5. Spoon the filling mixture evenly into the halved sweet peppers, pressing down gently to pack the filling.
6. Lightly spray the air fryer basket with olive oil spray.
7. Place the stuffed sweet peppers in the air fryer basket.
8. Air fry for 15-20 minutes until the peppers are tender and the filling is heated through and slightly golden on top.
9. Remove from the air fryer and let cool for a few minutes before serving.
10. Serve the Mediterranean stuffed sweet peppers hot.

INGREDIENTS

* 4 sweet peppers (any colour), halved and seeds removed
* 200g lean ground turkey or chicken
* 1 small onion, finely chopped
* 2 cloves garlic, minced
* 120g cooked quinoa
* 100g cherry tomatoes, diced
* 50g feta cheese, crumbled
* 30g chopped fresh parsley
* 1 tsp dried oregano
* Salt and pepper to taste
* Olive oil spray

Cal 200 | Fat 8 g | Carb 18 g | Protein 15 g | Serving 2 | Cook time 25 min

HERB-CRUSTED CHICKEN BREAST WITH ROASTED VEGETABLES

INGREDIENTS

- *2 boneless, skinless chicken breasts*
- *15ml olive oil*
- *1 tsp dried thyme*
- *1 tsp dried rosemary*
- *1 tsp dried oregano*
- *1/2 tsp garlic powder*
- *Salt and pepper to taste*
- *200g mixed vegetables (such as sweet peppers, courgette, and cherry tomatoes), chopped*

Cal 300 | Fat 9 g | Carb 20 g | Protein 16 g | Serving 2 | Cook time 30 min

INSTRUCTIONS

1. Preheat the air fryer to 200°C in the roast mode.
2. In a small bowl, mix together olive oil, dried thyme, dried rosemary, dried oregano, garlic powder, salt, and pepper to create the herb crust.
3. Pat dry the chicken breasts with paper towels and rub the herb crust mixture evenly over both sides of the chicken breasts.
4. Place the seasoned chicken breasts in the air fryer basket.
5. In a separate bowl, toss the mixed vegetables with a drizzle of olive oil, salt, and pepper.
6. Add the seasoned vegetables to the air fryer basket around the chicken breasts.
7. Air fry for 20-25 minutes, flipping the chicken breasts halfway through, until the chicken is cooked through and the vegetables are tender and slightly caramelized.
8. Remove from the air fryer and let rest for a few minutes before serving.
9. Serve the herb-crusted chicken breasts with roasted vegetables.

Lemon-Garlic Salmon with Asparagus Spears

INSTRUCTIONS

1. Preheat the air fryer to 200°C in the roast mode.
2. In a small bowl, mix together minced garlic, lemon zest, lemon juice, olive oil, salt, and pepper to create the marinade.
3. Place the salmon fillets and trimmed asparagus spears in a shallow dish and pour the marinade over them. Gently toss to coat.
4. Arrange the salmon fillets and asparagus spears in the air fryer basket in a single layer.
5. Air fry for 10-12 minutes, or until the salmon is cooked through and flakes easily with a fork, and the asparagus is tender-crisp.
6. Remove from the air fryer and let rest for a few minutes.
7. Garnish with fresh dill, if desired, before serving.
8. Serve the lemon-garlic salmon with asparagus spears hot.

INGREDIENTS

* 2 salmon fillets
* 200g asparagus spears, trimmed
* 2 cloves garlic, minced
* Zest and juice of 1 lemon
* 15ml olive oil
* Salt and pepper to taste
* Fresh dill for garnish (optional)

Cal 300 | Fat 18 g | Carb 7 g | Protein 25 g | Serving 2 | Cook time 20 min

QUINOA AND BLACK BEAN STUFFED COURGETTE BOATS

INGREDIENTS

* *2 large courgettes*
* *120g cooked quinoa*
* *200g canned black beans, drained and rinsed*
* *1/2 red sweet pepper, diced*
* *1/2 small onion, diced*
* *2 cloves garlic, minced*
* *1 tsp ground cumin*
* *1/2 tsp chili powder*
* *Salt and pepper to taste*
* *50g grated cheddar cheese (optional)*
* *Fresh cilantro for garnish (optional)*
* *Olive oil spray*

Cal 300 | Fat 18 g | Carb 8 g | Protein 25 g | Serving 2 | Cook time 20 min

INSTRUCTIONS

1. Preheat the air fryer to 180°C in the bake mode.
2. Slice each courgette in half lengthwise, then use a spoon to scoop out the flesh, leaving about 0.6 centimeters. thick shells. Reserve the scooped-out flesh for later use.
3. In a skillet over medium heat, sauté diced onion and minced garlic until softened.
4. Add diced red Sweet Pepper to the skillet and cook for another 2-3 min.
5. Stir in the cooked quinoa, black beans, reserved courgettes flesh, ground cumin, chili powder, salt, and pepper. Cook for 3-4 minutes until heated through and well combined.
6. Stuff each courgette boat with the quinoa and black bean mixture.
7. Lightly spray the air fryer basket with olive oil spray.
8. Place the stuffed courgette boats in the air fryer basket.
9. Air fry for 12-15 minutes, or until the courgette is tender and the filling is heated through.
10. If desired, sprinkle grated cheddar cheese over the top of each stuffed courgette boat during the last 5 minutes of cooking.
11. Remove from the air fryer and let cool for a few minutes.
12. Garnish with fresh cilantro before serving, if desired.
13. Serve the quinoa and black bean stuffed courgettes boats hot.

Turkey and Veggie Meatballs with Marinara Sauce

INSTRUCTIONS

1. Preheat the air fryer to 180°C in the bake mode.
2. In a large bowl, combine lean ground turkey, grated courgette, grated carrot, diced onion, minced garlic, chopped fresh parsley, gluten-free breadcrumbs, egg, dried oregano, dried basil, salt, and pepper. Mix until well combined.
3. Shape the turkey mixture into meatballs of desired size.
4. Lightly spray the air fryer basket with olive oil spray.
5. Place the meatballs in the air fryer basket, making sure they are not touching.
6. Air fry for 12-15 minutes until the meatballs are cooked through and golden brown on the outside, shaking the basket halfway through cooking.
7. Warm the marinara sauce in a small saucepan over low heat.
8. Serve the turkey and veggie meatballs with marinara sauce.

INGREDIENTS

- *250g lean ground turkey*
- *60g grated courgette, squeezed to remove excess moisture*
- *60g grated carrot*
- *60g diced onion*
- *2 cloves garlic, minced*
- *30g chopped fresh parsley*
- *60g gluten-free breadcrumbs*
- *1 egg*
- *1/2 tsp dried oregano*
- *1/2 tsp dried basil*
- *Salt and pepper to taste*
- *240ml marinara sauce*
- *Olive oil spray*

Cal 250 | Fat 9 g | Carb 20 g | Protein 20 g | Serving 2 | Cook time 25 min

CRISPY TOFU BUDDHA BOWL WITH SESAME DRESSING

INGREDIENTS

For Crispy Tofu:
- 200g firm tofu, drained and pressed
- 15g cornstarch
- 15ml soy sauce
- 5ml sesame oil
- 1/2 tsp garlic powder
- 1/2 tsp ground ginger
- Olive oil spray

For Buddha Bowl:
- 100g cooked quinoa
- 240g mixed salad greens
- 1/2 cucumber, sliced
- 1 carrot, shredded
- 60g red cabbage, thinly sliced
- 2 radishes, thinly sliced
- 1 avocado, sliced
- 15g sesame seeds, for garnish
- Fresh cilantro, for garnish

For Sesame Dressing:
- 30ml soy sauce
- 15ml rice vinegar
- 15ml sesame oil
- 5ml honey or maple syrup
- 5g grated ginger
- 1 garlic clove, minced

Cal 400 | Fat 20 g | Carb 45 g | Protein 15 g | Serving 2 | Cook time 25 min

INSTRUCTIONS

1. Preheat the air fryer to 200°C in the bake mode.
2. Cut the drained and pressed tofu into cubes.
3. In a bowl, toss the tofu cubes with cornstarch until coated.
4. In another bowl, mix together soy sauce, sesame oil, garlic powder, and ground ginger. Add the tofu cubes to the mixture and toss until evenly coated.
5. Arrange the tofu cubes in a single layer in the air fryer basket.
6. Lightly spray the tofu cubes with olive oil spray.
7. Air fry for 15-20 minutes until the tofu is crispy and golden brown, shaking the basket halfway through cooking.
8. Meanwhile, prepare the Buddha bowl by dividing cooked quinoa, mixed salad greens, sliced cucumber, shredded carrot, thinly sliced red cabbage, sliced radishes, and avocado slices among serving bowls.
9. To make the sesame dressing, whisk together soy sauce, rice vinegar, sesame oil, honey or maple syrup, grated ginger, and minced garlic in a small bowl.
10. Drizzle the sesame dressing over the Buddha bowls.
11. Once the tofu is crispy, remove it from the air fryer and add it to the Buddha bowls.
12. Garnish with sesame seeds and fresh cilantro, if desired.
13. Serve the crispy tofu Buddha bowls with sesame dressing immediately.

Spinach and Mushroom Quesadillas with Avocado Salsa

INSTRUCTIONS

1. In a skillet, heat olive oil over medium heat. Add sliced mushrooms and thinly sliced onion. Cook until mushrooms are tender and onions are translucent, about 5-7 minutes. Season with salt and pepper to taste. Remove from heat and set aside.
2. In a separate skillet, wilt spinach leaves over medium heat for about 2-3 minutes. Remove from heat and set aside.
3. To assemble the quesadillas, place a tortilla on a flat surface. Sprinkle shredded mozzarella cheese evenly over one half of the tortilla. Top with cooked spinach and mushroom mixture. Fold the other half of the tortilla over the filling to create a half-moon shape.
4. Preheat the air fryer to 180°C in the bake mode.
5. Lightly spray the air fryer basket with olive oil spray.
6. Carefully transfer the assembled quesadilla to the air fryer basket.
7. Air fry for 3-4 minutes on each side until the quesadilla is golden brown and crispy.
8. Meanwhile, prepare the avocado salsa by combining diced avocado, diced tomato, finely chopped red onion, chopped fresh cilantro, lime juice, salt, and pepper in a bowl. Mix well.
9. Once the quesadillas are cooked, remove from the air fryer and let cool for a minute.
10. Cut each quesadilla into wedges and serve hot with avocado salsa on the side.

INGREDIENTS

For Spinach and Mushroom Quesadillas:
- 4 whole wheat tortillas
- 200g spinach leaves
- 200g mushrooms, sliced
- 1 small onion, thinly sliced
- 100g shredded mozzarella cheese
- 15ml olive oil
- Salt and pepper to taste

For Avocado Salsa:
- 1 ripe avocado, diced
- 1 small tomato, diced
- 60g red onion, finely chopped
- 15g chopped fresh cilantro
- 15ml lime juice
- Salt and pepper to taste

Cal 300 | Fat 15 g | Carb 26 g | Protein 16 g | Serving 2 | Cook time 30 min

TERIYAKI CHICKEN AND BROCCOLI SKEWERS

INGREDIENTS

* *2 boneless, skinless chicken breasts, cut into cubes*
* *240g broccoli florets*
* *60ml teriyaki sauce (store-bought or homemade)*
* *15ml low-sodium soy sauce*
* *15ml honey or maple syrup*
* *1 clove garlic, minced*
* *5g grated ginger*
* *Olive oil spray*
* *Sesame seeds for garnish (optional)*
* *Sliced green onions for garnish (optional)*

Cal 250 | Fat 5 g | Carb 20 g | Protein 25 g | Serving 2 | Cook time 25 min

INSTRUCTIONS

1. In a bowl, whisk together teriyaki sauce, low-sodium soy sauce, honey or maple syrup, minced garlic, and grated ginger to make the marinade.
2. Add chicken cubes to the marinade and toss to coat. Cover and refrigerate for at least 30 minutes to marinate.
3. Preheat the air fryer to 200°C in the grill mode.
4. Thread marinated chicken cubes and broccoli florets onto skewers, alternating between chicken and broccoli.
5. Lightly spray the air fryer basket with olive oil spray.
6. Place the skewers in the air fryer basket in a single layer.
7. Grill for 10-12 minutes, turning halfway through cooking, until the chicken is cooked through and the broccoli is tender-crisp.
8. Remove from the air fryer and let cool for a few minutes.
9. Garnish with sesame seeds and sliced green onions, if desired.
10. Serve the teriyaki chicken and broccoli skewers hot.

Aubergine Parmesan with Fresh Tomato Sauce

INSTRUCTIONS

1. Preheat the air fryer to 200°C in the bake mode.
2. In a shallow dish, combine gluten free breadcrumbs, grated Parmesan cheese, dried oregano, dried basil, garlic powder, salt, and pepper to make the breading mixture.
3. Dip each aubergine slice into the beaten eggs, then coat both sides with the breadcrumb mixture, pressing gently to adhere.
4. Lightly spray the air fryer basket with olive oil spray.
5. Arrange the breaded aubergine slices in a single layer in the air fryer basket.
6. Air fry for 10-12 minutes until the aubergine is golden brown and crispy, flipping halfway through cooking.
7. Meanwhile, prepare the fresh tomato sauce by heating olive oil in a saucepan over medium heat. Add minced garlic and cook for 1 minute until fragrant.
8. Add diced tomatoes to the saucepan and cook for 5-7 minutes until softened, stirring occasionally.
9. Stir in chopped fresh basil and season with salt and pepper to taste.
10. Once the aubergine slices are crispy, remove them from the air fryer and serve hot with fresh tomato sauce spooned over the top.

INGREDIENTS

For Aubergine Parmesan:
* *1 large aubergine, sliced into 1.25cm rounds*
* *60g gluten-free breadcrumbs*
* *60g grated Parmesan cheese*
* *1 tsp dried oregano*
* *1 tsp dried basil*
* *1/2 tsp garlic powder*
* *Salt and pepper to taste*
* *2 eggs, beaten*
* *Olive oil spray*

For Fresh Tomato Sauce:
* *4 ripe tomatoes, diced*
* *2 cloves garlic, minced*
* *30g chopped fresh basil*
* *15ml olive oil*
* *Salt and pepper to taste*

Cal 250 | Fat 9 g | Carb 26 g | Protein 16 g | Serving 2 | Cook time 30 min

CHICKEN NUGGETS WITH CARROT STICKS

INSTRUCTIONS

1. Preheat the air fryer to 200°C in the bake mode.
2. In a shallow dish, combine gluten free breadcrumbs, grated Parmesan cheese, garlic powder, paprika, salt, and pepper to make the breading mixture.
3. Dip each chicken piece into the beaten egg, then coat with the breadcrumb mixture, pressing gently to adhere.
4. Place the breaded chicken nuggets in a single layer in the air fryer basket.
5. Lightly spray the chicken nuggets with olive oil spray.
6. In a separate bowl, toss carrot sticks with olive oil, dried thyme, salt, and pepper until coated.
7. Arrange the seasoned carrot sticks in the air fryer basket around the chicken nuggets.
8. Air fry for 10-12 minutes, flipping the chicken nuggets halfway through cooking, until golden brown and crispy, and the carrots are tender.
9. Remove from the air fryer and let cool for a minute before serving.
10. Serve the air fryer chicken nuggets with carrot sticks hot.

INGREDIENTS

For Chicken Nuggets:

* *2 boneless, skinless chicken breasts, cut into bite-sized pieces*
* *120g gluten free breadcrumbs*
* *30g grated Parmesan cheese*
* *1/2 tsp garlic powder*
* *1/2 tsp paprika*
* *Salt and pepper to taste*
* *1 egg, beaten*
* *Olive oil spray*

For Carrot Sticks:

* *2 large carrots, peeled and cut into sticks*
* *15ml olive oil*
* *1/2 tsp dried thyme*
* *Salt and pepper to taste*

Cal 250 | Fat 9 g | Carb 20 g | Protein 20 g | Serving 2 | Cook time 25 min

APPETIZERS AND SIDE DISHES

GARLIC PARMESAN ROASTED BRUSSELS SPROUTS

INGREDIENTS

* 500g Brussels sprouts, trimmed and halved
* 30g olive oil
* 2 cloves garlic, minced
* 60g grated Parmesan cheese
* Salt and pepper to taste

Cal 150 | Fat 7 g | Carb 12 g | Protein 8 g | Serving 2 | Cook time 20 min

INSTRUCTIONS

1. Preheat the air fryer to 200°C in the roast mode.
2. In a large bowl, toss Brussels sprouts with olive oil, minced garlic, grated Parmesan cheese, salt, and pepper until evenly coated.
3. Arrange the Brussels sprouts in a single layer in the air fryer basket.
4. Air fry for 12-15 minutes, shaking the basket halfway through cooking, until the Brussels sprouts are golden brown and crispy on the outside, and tender on the inside.
5. Remove from the air fryer and transfer to a serving dish.
6. Serve the garlic Parmesan roasted Brussels sprouts hot as a delicious side dish.

Sweet Potato Wedges

INSTRUCTIONS

1. Preheat the air fryer to 200°C in the roast mode.
2. In a large bowl, toss sweet potato wedges with olive oil, paprika, garlic powder, onion powder, dried thyme, salt, and pepper until evenly coated.
3. Arrange the sweet potato wedges in a single layer in the air fryer basket.
4. Air fry for 15-20 minutes, flipping the wedges halfway through cooking, until the sweet potatoes are golden brown and crispy on the outside, and tender on the inside.
5. Remove from the air fryer and transfer to a serving dish.
6. Serve the air fryer sweet potato wedges hot as a delightful appetizer or side dish.

INGREDIENTS

* *2 medium sweet potatoes, washed and cut into wedges*
* *30ml olive oil*
* *1 tsp paprika*
* *1/2 tsp garlic powder*
* *1/2 tsp onion powder*
* *1/2 tsp dried thyme*
* *Salt and pepper to taste*

Cal 150 | Fat 7 g | Carb 20 g | Protein 2 g | Serving 2 | Cook time 20 min

CRISPY BAKED COURGETTE FRIES

INSTRUCTIONS

1. Preheat the air fryer to 200°C in the bake mode.
2. In a shallow dish, combine gluten-free breadcrumbs, grated Parmesan cheese, garlic powder, paprika, salt, and pepper to make the breading mixture.
3. Dip each courgette strip into the beaten egg, then coat with the breadcrumb mixture, pressing gently to adhere.
4. Place the breaded courgette fries in a single layer in the air fryer basket.
5. Lightly spray the courgette fries with olive oil spray.
6. Air fry for 10-12 minutes until the courgette fries are golden brown and crispy, shaking the basket halfway through cooking.
7. Remove from the air fryer and let cool for a minute before serving.
8. Serve the crispy baked courgette fries hot with your favourite dipping sauce.

INGREDIENTS

- *2 medium courgettes, cut into thin strips*
- *120g gluten-free breadcrumbs*
- *60g grated Parmesan cheese*
- *1/2 tsp garlic powder*
- *1/2 tsp paprika*
- *Salt and pepper to taste*
- *1 egg, beaten*
- *Olive oil spray*

Cal 150 | Fat 5 g | Carb 20 g | Protein 8 g | Serving 2 | Cook time 20 min

SPICY BUFFALO CAULIFLOWER BITES

INSTRUCTIONS

1. Preheat the air fryer to 200°C in the roast mode.
2. In a large bowl, whisk together almond flour, water, garlic powder, paprika, onion powder, cayenne pepper, salt, and pepper to make the batter.
3. Add cauliflower florets to the batter and toss until evenly coated.
4. Lightly spray the air fryer basket with olive oil spray.
5. Place the coated cauliflower florets in a single layer in the air fryer basket, shaking off any excess batter.
6. Air fry for 15-20 minutes, shaking the basket halfway through cooking, until the cauliflower is golden brown and crispy.
7. In a separate bowl, mix hot sauce and melted butter to make the buffalo sauce.
8. Once the cauliflower is cooked, transfer it to a large bowl and toss with the buffalo sauce until evenly coated.
9. Serve the spicy buffalo cauliflower bites hot with ranch or blue cheese dressing for dipping.

INGREDIENTS

- *1 head cauliflower, cut into florets*
- *120g almond flour*
- *120ml water*
- *1 tsp garlic powder*
- *1 tsp paprika*
- *1/2 tsp onion powder*
- *1 g cayenne pepper (adjust to taste)*
- *Salt and pepper to taste*
- *60ml hot sauce (such as Frank's RedHot)*
- *30g unsalted butter, melted*
- *Olive oil spray*

Cal 150 | Fat 7 g | Carb 20 g | Protein 4 g | Serving 2 | Cook time 25 min

HERB-ROASTED CHICKPEAS

INSTRUCTIONS

1. Preheat the air fryer to 200°C in the roast mode.
2. Pat dry the chickpeas with a clean kitchen towel to remove excess moisture.
3. In a bowl, toss chickpeas with olive oil, dried thyme, dried rosemary, garlic powder, paprika, salt, and pepper until evenly coated.
4. Arrange the seasoned chickpeas in a single layer in the air fryer basket.
5. Air fry for 15-20 minutes, shaking the basket halfway through cooking, until the chickpeas are golden brown and crispy.
6. Remove from the air fryer and let cool for a few minutes.
7. Serve the herb-roasted chickpeas as a crunchy and flavorful snack.

INGREDIENTS

* 1 can (400g) chickpeas, drained and rinsed
* 15ml olive oil
* 1 tsp dried thyme
* 1 tsp dried rosemary
* 1 tsp garlic powder
* 1/2 tsp paprika
* Salt and pepper to taste

Cal 150 | Fat 5 g | Carb 20 g | Protein 6 g | Serving 2 | Cook time 25 min

Lemon-Garlic Green Beans

INSTRUCTIONS

1. Preheat the air fryer to 180°C in the roast mode.
2. In a bowl, toss green beans with minced garlic, lemon zest, lemon juice, olive oil, salt, and pepper until evenly coated.
3. Arrange the seasoned green beans in a single layer in the air fryer basket.
4. Air fry for 8-10 minutes until the green beans are tender-crisp and slightly charred, shaking the basket halfway through cooking.
5. Remove from the air fryer and transfer to a serving dish.
6. Serve the lemon-garlic green beans hot as a zesty and flavorful side dish.

INGREDIENTS

- *300g green beans, trimmed*
- *2 cloves garlic, minced*
- *Zest of 1 lemon*
- *15ml lemon juice*
- *15ml olive oil*
- *Salt and pepper to taste*

Cal 70 | Fat 4 g | Carb 8 g | Protein 2 g | Serving 2 | Cook time 15 min

MEDITERRANEAN STUFFED MUSHROOMS

INGREDIENTS

- *8 large mushrooms, stems removed and cleaned*
- *120g cooked quinoa*
- *60g chopped sun-dried tomatoes*
- *60g crumbled feta cheese*
- *30g chopped fresh parsley*
- *15 g chopped fresh basil*
- *1 clove garlic, minced*
- *15ml olive oil*
- *Salt and pepper to taste*

Cal 80 | Fat 5 g | Carb 6 g | Protein 4 g | Serving 2 | Cook time 15 min

INSTRUCTIONS

1. Preheat the air fryer to 180°C in the roast mode.
2. In a bowl, mix together cooked quinoa, chopped sun-dried tomatoes, crumbled feta cheese, chopped fresh parsley, chopped fresh basil, minced garlic, olive oil, salt, and pepper.
3. Stuff each mushroom cap with the quinoa mixture, pressing gently to pack the filling.
4. Arrange the stuffed mushrooms in the air fryer basket.
5. Air fry for 10-12 minutes until the mushrooms are tender and the filling is heated through.
6. Remove from the air fryer and let cool for a minute.
7. Serve the Mediterranean stuffed mushrooms hot as a delightful appetizer or side dish.

CRISPY AIR FRYER KALE CHIPS

INSTRUCTIONS

1. Preheat the air fryer to 160°C in the roast mode.
2. In a large bowl, toss kale pieces with olive oil, garlic powder, onion powder, paprika, and salt until evenly coated.
3. Arrange the seasoned kale pieces in a single layer in the air fryer basket.
4. Air fry for 5-7 minutes until the kale is crispy and slightly browned, shaking the basket halfway through cooking.
5. Remove from the air fryer and let cool for a minute.
6. Serve the crispy air fryer kale chips immediately as a healthy and crunchy snack.

INGREDIENTS

* *1 bunch kale, stems removed and torn into bite-sized pieces*
* *15ml olive oil*
* *1/2 tsp garlic powder*
* *1/2 tsp onion powder*
* *1 g paprika*
* *Salt to taste*

Cal 50 | Fat 3 g | Carb 5 g | Protein 2 g | Serving 2 | Cook time 10 min

SOUTHWEST QUINOA SALAD CUPS

INGREDIENTS

* *180g cooked quinoa*
* *100g black beans, rinsed and drained*
* *100g corn kernels (fresh, canned, or frozen)*
* *1/2 red sweet pepper, diced*
* *60g diced red onion*
* *15g chopped fresh cilantro*
* *1 avocado, diced*
* *Juice of 1 lime*
* *15ml olive oil*
* *1/2 tsp ground cumin*
* *1 g chili powder*
* *Salt and pepper to taste*
* *Lettuce leaves, for serving*

Cal 200 | Fat 9 g | Carb 20 g | Protein 6 g | Serving 2 | Cook time 15 min

INSTRUCTIONS

1. In a large bowl, combine cooked quinoa, black beans, corn kernels, diced red sweet pepper, diced red onion, chopped fresh cilantro, and diced avocado.
2. In a small bowl, whisk together lime juice, olive oil, ground cumin, chili powder, salt, and pepper to make the dressing.
3. Pour the dressing over the quinoa salad mixture and toss until well combined.
4. Preheat the air fryer to 180°C in the bake mode.
5. Place lettuce leaves in muffin cups to create cups for serving.
6. Spoon the quinoa salad mixture into the lettuce cups.
7. Air fry for 5-7 minutes until the lettuce cups are slightly crispy.
8. Remove from the air fryer and let cool for a minute before serving.
9. Serve the Southwest quinoa salad cups as a nutritious and flavorful appetizer or side dish.

Caprese Skewers with Balsamic Glaze

INSTRUCTIONS

1. Thread one cherry tomato, one mozzarella ball, and one basil leaf onto each skewer, repeating until all ingredients are used.
2. Preheat the air fryer to 180°C in the roast mode.
3. Place the assembled skewers in the air fryer basket in a single layer.
4. Air fry for 3-4 minutes until the mozzarella starts to soften and the tomatoes are slightly blistered.
5. Remove from the air fryer and let cool for a minute.
6. Arrange the Caprese skewers on a serving platter.
7. Drizzle balsamic glaze over the skewers just before serving.
8. Serve the Caprese skewers with balsamic glaze as a delightful and elegant appetizer.

INGREDIENTS

* *12 cherry tomatoes*
* *12 small fresh mozzarella balls (bocconcini)*
* *12 fresh basil leaves*
* *Balsamic glaze, for drizzling*
* *Wooden skewers*

Cal 80 | Fat 6 g | Carb 2 g | Protein 5 g | Serving 2 | Cook time 10 min

FISH AND SEAFOOD

Lemon Herb Salmon

INSTRUCTIONS

1. Preheat the air fryer to 180°C in the bake mode.
2. In a small bowl, mix together melted butter, minced garlic, chopped fresh parsley, chopped fresh dill, lemon zest, lemon juice, salt, and pepper to make the herb butter mixture.
3. Place salmon fillets on a parchment-lined tray or directly in the air fryer basket.
4. Brush the herb butter mixture over the salmon fillets, coating them evenly.
5. Air fry for 10-12 minutes, depending on the thickness of the salmon, until the salmon is cooked through and flakes easily with a fork.
6. Remove from the air fryer and let rest for a minute before serving.
7. Serve the lemon herb butter air fryer salmon hot with your favourite side dishes.

INGREDIENTS

* *2 salmon fillets (about 150g each)*
* *30g unsalted butter, melted*
* *2 cloves garlic, minced*
* *15g chopped fresh parsley*
* *15g chopped fresh dill*
* *Zest of 1 lemon*
* *Juice of 1/2 lemon*
* *Salt and pepper to taste*

Cal 250 | Fat 15 g | Carb 1 g | Protein 25 g | Serving 2 | Cook time 15 min

GARLIC PARMESAN SHRIMP

INGREDIENTS

* *300g large shrimp, peeled and deveined*
* *30ml olive oil*
* *2 cloves garlic, minced*
* *60g grated Parmesan cheese*
* *15ml chopped fresh parsley*
* *Salt and pepper to taste*
* *Lemon wedges for serving (optional)*

Cal 250 | Fat 15 g | Carb 2 g | Protein 25 g | Serving 2 | Cook time 15 min

INSTRUCTIONS

1. Preheat the air fryer to 200°C in the bake mode.
2. In a bowl, toss the shrimp with olive oil, minced garlic, grated Parmesan cheese, chopped fresh parsley, salt, and pepper until evenly coated.
3. Place the shrimp in the air fryer basket in a single layer.
4. Air fry for 5-7 minutes, shaking the basket halfway through cooking, until the shrimp are pink and cooked through.
5. Remove from the air fryer and transfer to a serving plate.
6. Serve the garlic Parmesan air fryer shrimp hot with lemon wedges on the side, if desired.

Cajun Blackened Tilapia

INSTRUCTIONS

1. Preheat the air fryer to 200°C in the bake mode.
2. In a small bowl, mix together olive oil, Cajun seasoning, garlic powder, onion powder, paprika, dried thyme, salt, and pepper to make the blackened seasoning.
3. Pat dry the tilapia fillets with a paper towel.
4. Rub the blackened seasoning mixture evenly over both sides of the tilapia fillets.
5. Place the seasoned tilapia fillets in the air fryer basket in a single layer.
6. Air fry for 8-10 minutes, flipping the fillets halfway through cooking, until the tilapia is cooked through and flakes easily with a fork.
7. Remove from the air fryer and let rest for a minute before serving.
8. Serve the Cajun blackened air fryer tilapia hot with lemon wedges on the side, if desired.

INGREDIENTS

- 2 tilapia fillets (about 150g each)
- 15ml olive oil
- 15g Cajun seasoning
- 1/2 tsp garlic powder
- 1/2 tsp onion powder
- 1 g paprika
- 1 g dried thyme
- Salt and pepper to taste
- Lemon wedges for serving (optional)

Cal 200 | Fat 9 g | Carb 2 g | Protein 25 g | Serving 2 | Cook time 15 min

HERB-CRUSTED COD

INSTRUCTIONS

1. Preheat the air fryer to 200°C in the bake mode.
2. In a small bowl, mix together gluten-free breadcrumbs, grated Parmesan cheese, chopped fresh parsley, chopped fresh dill, garlic powder, onion powder, salt, and pepper to make the herb crust.
3. Pat dry the cod fillets with a paper towel.
4. Brush the cod fillets with olive oil on both sides.
5. Press the herb crust mixture onto both sides of the cod fillets, ensuring they are evenly coated.
6. Place the coated cod fillets in the air fryer basket in a single layer.
7. Air fry for 10-12 minutes, depending on the thickness of the cod fillets, until the fish is opaque and flakes easily with a fork.
8. Remove from the air fryer and let rest for a minute before serving.
9. Serve the herb-crusted air fryer cod hot with lemon wedges on the side, if desired.

INGREDIENTS

* 2 cod fillets (about 150g each)
* 15ml olive oil
* 2 tbsp gluten-free breadcrumbs
* 15g grated Parmesan cheese
* 5g chopped fresh parsley
* 5g chopped fresh dill
* 1/2 tsp garlic powder
* 0.5 g onion powder
* Salt and pepper to taste
* Lemon wedges for serving (optional)

Cal 200 | Fat 9 g | Carb 3 g | Protein 25 g | Serving 2 | Cook time 15 min

Teriyaki Glazed Mahi Mahi

INSTRUCTIONS

1. Preheat the air fryer to 200°C in the bake mode.
2. In a small saucepan over medium heat, combine low-sodium soy sauce, honey or maple syrup, rice vinegar, minced garlic, and grated ginger. Bring to a simmer.
3. In a small bowl, mix cornstarch with water until dissolved to make a slurry. Add the slurry to the saucepan and cook, stirring constantly, until the sauce thickens, about 1-2 minutes. Remove from heat.
4. Pat dry the Mahi Mahi fillets with a paper towel.
5. Brush the teriyaki glaze over both sides of the Mahi Mahi fillets, reserving some for serving.
6. Place the glazed Mahi Mahi fillets in the air fryer basket in a single layer.
7. Air fry for 10-12 minutes, depending on the thickness of the Mahi Mahi fillets, until the fish is cooked through and flakes easily with a fork.
8. Remove from the air fryer and let rest for a minute before serving.
9. Serve the teriyaki glazed air fryer Mahi Mahi hot, garnished with sesame seeds, chopped green onions, and extra teriyaki glaze on the side, if desired.

INGREDIENTS

* 2 Mahi Mahi fillets (about 150g each)
* 30ml low-sodium soy sauce
* 15ml honey or maple syrup
* 15ml rice vinegar
* 1 clove garlic, minced
* 2.5g grated ginger
* 1/2 tsp cornstarch
* 7.5ml water
* Sesame seeds and chopped green onions for garnish (optional)

Cal 200 | Fat 5 g | Carb 8 g | Protein 25 g | Serving 2 | Cook time 15 min

COCONUT-CRUSTED PRAWNS

INGREDIENTS

* *200g large prawns, peeled and deveined*
* *60g shredded coconut*
* *30g gluten-free breadcrumbs*
* *1/2 tsp garlic powder*
* *1/2 tsp paprika*
* *1/2 tsp salt*
* *1 g black pepper*
* *1 egg, beaten*
* *Cooking spray*

Cal 250 | Fat 15 g | Carb 8 g | Protein 15 g | Serving 2 | Cook time 15 min

INSTRUCTIONS

1. Preheat the air fryer to 200°C in the bake mode.
2. In a shallow bowl, mix together shredded coconut, panko breadcrumbs, garlic powder, paprika, salt, and black pepper.
3. Dip each prawn into the beaten egg, then coat with the coconut mixture, pressing gently to adhere.
4. Place the coated prawns in the air fryer basket in a single layer.
5. Lightly spray the prawns with cooking spray.
6. Air fry for 6-8 minutes, flipping the prawns halfway through cooking, until golden brown and crispy.
7. Remove from the air fryer and let cool for a minute before serving.
8. Serve the coconut-crusted air fryer prawns hot with your favourite dipping sauce.

MEDITERRANEAN HERB SEA BASS WITH CHEESE

INSTRUCTIONS

1. Preheat the air fryer to 200°C in the bake mode.
2. In a small bowl, mix together olive oil, minced garlic, chopped fresh parsley, chopped fresh basil, dried oregano, dried thyme, salt, and pepper to make the herb mixture.
3. Pat dry the sea bass fillets with a paper towel.
4. Brush the herb mixture over both sides of the sea bass fillets, coating them evenly.
5. Sprinkle grated Parmesan cheese over the top of each sea bass fillet.
6. Place the seasoned sea bass fillets in the air fryer basket in a single layer.
7. Air fry for 10-12 minutes, depending on the thickness of the sea bass fillets, until the fish is opaque and flakes easily with a fork and the cheese is golden brown and bubbly.
8. Remove from the air fryer and let rest for a minute before serving.
9. Serve the Mediterranean herb air fryer sea bass with cheese hot with lemon wedges on the side, if desired.

INGREDIENTS

- 2 sea bass fillets (about 150g each)
- 30ml olive oil
- 2 cloves garlic, minced
- 5g chopped fresh parsley
- 5g chopped fresh basil
- 1/2 tsp dried oregano
- 1/2 tsp dried thyme
- Salt and pepper to taste
- 30g grated Parmesan cheese
- Lemon wedges for serving (optional)

Cal 300 | Fat 20 g | Carb 2 g | Protein 25 g | Serving 2 | Cook time 15 min

CHILI LIME SCALLOPS

INSTRUCTIONS

1. Preheat the air fryer to 200°C in the bake mode.
2. In a bowl, combine olive oil, lime zest, lime juice, chili powder, garlic powder, paprika, salt, and pepper.
3. Add the scallops to the bowl and toss until evenly coated with the marinade.
4. Place the scallops in the air fryer basket in a single layer.
5. Air fry for 5-7 minutes, flipping the scallops halfway through cooking, until they are opaque and slightly browned on the edges.
6. Remove from the air fryer and let cool for a minute.
7. Garnish with chopped fresh cilantro, if desired, and serve with lime wedges on the side.

INGREDIENTS

- *200g scallops, patted dry*
- *30ml olive oil*
- *Zest of 1 lime*
- *Juice of 1 lime*
- *1 tsp chili powder*
- *1/2 tsp garlic powder*
- *1/2 tsp paprika*
- *Salt and pepper to taste*
- *Chopped fresh cilantro for garnish (optional)*
- *Lime wedges for serving (optional)*

Cal 150 | Fat 8 g | Carb 2 g | Protein 20 g | Serving 2 | Cook time 10 min

SESAME GINGER TUNA STEAKS

INSTRUCTIONS

1. Preheat the air fryer to 200°C in the bake mode.
2. In a bowl, whisk together low-sodium soy sauce, sesame oil, rice vinegar, honey or maple syrup, grated ginger, and minced garlic to make the marinade.
3. Place the tuna steaks in a shallow dish and pour the marinade over them, ensuring they are evenly coated. Let marinate for 15-30 minutes.
4. Remove the tuna steaks from the marinade and sprinkle sesame seeds over both sides of the steaks, pressing gently to adhere.
5. Place the sesame ginger tuna steaks in the air fryer basket in a single layer.
6. Air fry for 5-7 minutes for medium-rare or 8-10 minutes for medium, flipping the steaks halfway through cooking.
7. Remove from the air fryer and let rest for a minute.
8. Garnish with chopped green onions, if desired, and serve hot.

INGREDIENTS

- 2 tuna steaks (about 150g each)
- 30ml low-sodium soy sauce
- 15ml sesame oil
- 15ml rice vinegar
- 15ml honey or maple syrup
- 5g grated ginger
- 1 clove garlic, minced
- 15g sesame seeds
- Chopped green onions for garnish (optional)

Cal 250 | Fat 9 g | Carb 5 g | Protein 16 g | Serving 2 | Cook time 10 min

LEMON PEPPER HADDOCK WITH TOMATOES AND MOZZARELLA

INGREDIENTS

* *2 haddock fillets (about 150g each)*
* *30ml olive oil*
* *Zest of 1 lemon*
* *5ml lemon pepper seasoning*
* *1/2 tsp garlic powder*
* *1/2 tsp onion powder*
* *Salt to taste*
* *2 medium tomatoes, sliced*
* *100g fresh mozzarella cheese, sliced*
* *Fresh basil leaves for garnish (optional)*
* *Lemon wedges for serving (optional)*

Cal 350 | Fat 20 g | Carb 5 g | Protein 16 g | Serving 2 | Cook time 20 min

INSTRUCTIONS

1. Preheat the air fryer to 200°C in the bake mode.
2. In a small bowl, mix together olive oil, lemon zest, lemon pepper seasoning, garlic powder, onion powder, and salt to make the seasoning mixture.
3. Pat dry the haddock fillets with a paper towel.
4. Brush the seasoning mixture over both sides of the haddock fillets, coating them evenly.
5. Place the seasoned haddock fillets in the air fryer basket in a single layer.
6. Air fry for 8 minutes.
7. Remove the haddock fillets from the air fryer and top each fillet with sliced tomatoes and mozzarella cheese.
8. Return the topped fillets to the air fryer and air fry for an additional 4-5 minutes, until the cheese is melted and bubbly.
9. Remove from the air fryer and let rest for a minute before serving.
10. Garnish with fresh basil leaves, if desired, and serve the crispy lemon pepper air fryer haddock with tomatoes and mozzarella hot, with lemon wedges on the side.

POULTRY RECIPES

GARLIC PARMESAN CHICKEN THIGHS

INGREDIENTS

- *4 bone-in, skin-on chicken thighs*
- *30ml olive oil*
- *2 cloves garlic, minced*
- *30g grated Parmesan cheese*
- *1 tsp dried parsley*
- *1/2 tsp garlic powder*
- *1/2 tsp onion powder*
- *Salt and pepper to taste*
- *Cooking spray*

Cal 350 | Fat 25 g | Carb 1 g | Protein 25 g | Serving 2 | Cook time 30 min

INSTRUCTIONS

1. Preheat the air fryer to 200°C in the bake mode.
2. In a small bowl, mix together olive oil, minced garlic, grated Parmesan cheese, dried parsley, garlic powder, onion powder, salt, and pepper to make the seasoning mixture.
3. Pat dry the chicken thighs with a paper towel.
4. Rub the seasoning mixture over both sides of the chicken thighs, coating them evenly.
5. Lightly spray the air fryer basket with cooking spray.
6. Place the seasoned chicken thighs in the air fryer basket, skin side up, in a single layer.
7. Air fry for 25-30 minutes, flipping the chicken thighs halfway through cooking, until they are golden brown and cooked through, with an internal temperature of 75°C (165°F).
8. Remove from the air fryer and let rest for a minute before serving.
9. Serve the garlic Parmesan air fryer chicken thighs hot with your favourite side dishes.

Lemon Herb Turkey Cutlets

INSTRUCTIONS

1. Preheat the air fryer to 200°C in the bake mode.
2. In a small bowl, whisk together olive oil, lemon zest, lemon juice, dried thyme, dried rosemary, garlic powder, onion powder, salt, and pepper to make the marinade.
3. Pat dry the turkey breasts with a paper towel and pound them into cutlets of even thickness.
4. Place the turkey cutlets in the marinade and toss until evenly coated. Let marinate for 15-30 minutes.
5. Remove the turkey cutlets from the marinade and shake off any excess.
6. Place the turkey cutlets in the air fryer basket in a single layer.
7. Air fry for 10-12 minutes, flipping the cutlets halfway through cooking, until they are cooked through and golden brown.
8. Remove from the air fryer and let rest for a minute before serving.
9. Serve the lemon herb air fryer turkey homemade cutlets hot with lemon wedges on the side, if desired.

INGREDIENTS

* *2 turkey breasts (about 200g each), pounded into cutlets*
* *30ml olive oil*
* *Zest of 1 lemon*
* *Juice of 1 lemon*
* *1 tsp dried thyme*
* *1 tsp dried rosemary*
* *1/2 tsp garlic powder*
* *1/2 tsp onion powder*
* *Salt and pepper to taste*
* *Lemon wedges for serving (optional)*

Cal 250 | Fat 9 g | Carb 1 g | Protein 16 g | Serving 2 | Cook time 25 min

CAJUN SPICED CHICKEN WINGS

INSTRUCTIONS

1. Preheat the air fryer to 200°C in the bake mode.
2. In a large bowl, toss the chicken wings with olive oil until evenly coated.
3. In a separate small bowl, mix together Cajun seasoning, garlic powder, onion powder, smoked paprika, cayenne pepper, and salt.
4. Sprinkle the spice mixture over the chicken wings and toss until they are evenly coated.
5. Place the seasoned chicken wings in the air fryer basket in a single layer, making sure they are not overcrowded.
6. Air fry for 25-30 minutes, flipping the wings halfway through cooking, until they are crispy and golden brown.
7. Remove from the air fryer and let rest for a minute before serving.
8. Serve the Cajun spiced air fryer chicken wings hot with lemon wedges and ranch or blue cheese dressing on the side for dipping, if desired.

INGREDIENTS

- 10 chicken wings, split into flats and drumettes
- 30ml olive oil
- 15ml Cajun seasoning
- 1/2 tsp garlic powder
- 1/2 tsp onion powder
- 1/2 tsp smoked paprika
- 1g cayenne pepper (adjust to taste)
- Salt to taste
- Lemon wedges for serving (optional)
- Ranch or blue cheese dressing for dipping (optional)

Cal 250 | Fat 18 g | Carb 2 g | Protein 20 g | Serving 2 | Cook time 30 min

Honey Mustard Chicken Drumsticks

INSTRUCTIONS

1. Preheat the air fryer to 200°C in the bake mode.
2. In a small bowl, whisk together honey, Dijon mustard, olive oil, minced garlic, paprika, salt, and pepper to make the marinade.
3. Pat dry the chicken drumsticks with a paper towel.
4. Place the chicken drumsticks in the marinade and toss until evenly coated. Let marinate for 15-30 minutes.
5. Remove the chicken drumsticks from the marinade and shake off any excess.
6. Place the chicken drumsticks in the air fryer basket in a single layer.
7. Air fry for 25-30 minutes, flipping the drumsticks halfway through cooking, until they are cooked through and golden brown.
8. Remove from the air fryer and let rest for a minute before serving.
9. Serve the honey mustard air fryer chicken drumsticks hot with lemon wedges on the side, if desired.

INGREDIENTS

- *6 chicken drumsticks*
- *30g honey*
- *30g Dijon mustard*
- *15ml olive oil*
- *1 clove garlic, minced*
- *1/2 tsp paprika*
- *Salt and pepper to taste*
- *Lemon wedges for serving (optional)*

Cal 300 | Fat 15 g | Carb 8 g | Protein 25 g | Serving 2 | Cook time 30 min

ROSEMARY BALSAMIC CORNISH HENS

INGREDIENTS

* *2 Cornish hens (about 500g each)*
* *30ml balsamic vinegar*
* *30ml olive oil*
* *2 cloves garlic, minced*
* *15g chopped fresh rosemary*
* *1/2 tsp dried thyme*
* *Salt and pepper to taste*
* *Lemon wedges for serving (optional)*

Cal 400 | Fat 25 g | Carb 5 g | Protein 16 g | Serving 2 | Cook time 40 min

INSTRUCTIONS

1. Preheat the air fryer to 200°C in the bake mode.
2. In a small bowl, whisk together balsamic vinegar, olive oil, minced garlic, chopped fresh rosemary, dried thyme, salt, and pepper to make the marinade.
3. Pat dry the Cornish hens with a paper towel.
4. Place the Cornish hens in a large ziplock bag or a shallow dish and pour the marinade over them, ensuring they are evenly coated. Let marinate for 1-2 hours in the refrigerator.
5. Remove the Cornish hens from the marinade and shake off any excess.
6. Place the Cornish hens in the air fryer basket, breast side down, in a single layer.
7. Air fry for 20 minutes.
8. Flip the Cornish hens and air fry for an additional 15-20 minutes, until they are cooked through and golden brown, and the internal temperature reaches 75°C (165°F).
9. Remove from the air fryer and let rest for a few minutes before serving.
10. Serve the rosemary balsamic air fryer Cornish hens hot with lemon wedges on the side, if desired.

Paprika Crusted Chicken Tenders

INSTRUCTIONS

1. Preheat the air fryer to 200°C in the bake mode.
2. In a small bowl, mix together olive oil, paprika, garlic powder, onion powder, dried oregano, salt, and pepper to make the seasoning mixture.
3. Pat dry the chicken breast tenders with a paper towel.
4. Brush the seasoning mixture over both sides of the chicken tenders, coating them evenly.
5. Place the seasoned chicken tenders in the air fryer basket in a single layer.
6. Air fry for 10-12 minutes, flipping the tenders halfway through cooking, until they are golden brown and cooked through.
7. Remove from the air fryer and let rest for a minute before serving.
8. Serve the paprika crusted air fryer chicken tenders hot with lemon wedges on the side, if desired.

INGREDIENTS

* *300g chicken breast tenders*
* *30ml olive oil*
* *1 tsp paprika*
* *1/2 tsp garlic powder*
* *1/2 tsp onion powder*
* *1/2 tsp dried oregano*
* *Salt and pepper to taste*
* *Lemon wedges for serving (optional)*

Cal 300 | Fat 15 g | Carb 2 g | Protein 25 g | Serving 2 | Cook time 15 min

MEDITERRANEAN HERB QUAIL

INGREDIENTS

* 4 quail, cleaned and patted dry
* 30ml olive oil
* 2 cloves garlic, minced
* 1 tsp chopped fresh rosemary
* 1 tsp chopped fresh thyme
* 1 tsp chopped fresh parsley
* 1/2 tsp dried oregano
* Salt and pepper to taste
* Lemon wedges for serving (optional)

Cal 300 | Fat 20 g | Carb 1 g | Protein 25 g | Serving 2 | Cook time 20 min

INSTRUCTIONS

1. Preheat the air fryer to 200°C in the bake mode.
2. In a small bowl, mix together olive oil, minced garlic, chopped fresh rosemary, chopped fresh thyme, chopped fresh parsley, dried oregano, salt, and pepper to make the herb mixture.
3. Pat dry the quail with a paper towel.
4. Rub the herb mixture over both sides of the quail, coating them evenly.
5. Place the seasoned quail in the air fryer basket in a single layer.
6. Air fry for 12-15 minutes, flipping the quail halfway through cooking, until they are golden brown and cooked through.
7. Remove from the air fryer and let rest for a minute before serving.
8. Serve the Mediterranean herb air fryer quail hot with lemon wedges on the side, if desired.

SPICY SRIRACHA TURKEY BURGERS

INSTRUCTIONS

1. Preheat the air fryer to 200°C in the bake mode.
2. In a large bowl, combine ground turkey, Sriracha sauce, breadcrumbs, egg, garlic powder, onion powder, paprika, salt, and pepper. Mix until well combined.
3. Divide the mixture into 2 portions and shape each portion into a burger patty.
4. Lightly spray the air fryer basket with cooking spray.
5. Place the turkey burger patties in the air fryer basket in a single layer.
6. Air fry for 10-12 minutes, flipping the burgers halfway through cooking, until they are cooked through and golden brown.
7. Remove from the air fryer and let rest for a minute before serving.
8. Serve the spicy Sriracha air fryer turkey burgers hot with your favourite toppings and side dishes.

INGREDIENTS

- *250g ground turkey*
- *15ml Sriracha sauce*
- *30g gluten-free breadcrumbs*
- *1 egg*
- *1/2 tsp garlic powder*
- *1/2 tsp onion powder*
- *1/2 tsp paprika*
- *Salt and pepper to taste*
- *Cooking spray*

Cal 250 | Fat 9 g | Carb 8 g | Protein 25 g | Serving 2 | Cook time 20 min

CHICKEN FILLET ROLLS STUFFED WITH ASPARAGUS AND CHEESE

INGREDIENTS

- *2 chicken breast fillets*
- *6 asparagus spears, trimmed*
- *50g cheese (such as mozzarella or cheddar), sliced*
- *Salt and pepper to taste*
- *15ml olive oil*
- *1/2 tsp garlic powder*
- *1/2 tsp dried thyme*
- *Cooking twine or toothpicks*

Cal 300 | Fat 15 g | Carb 5 g | Protein 35 g | Serving 2 | Cook time 25 min

INSTRUCTIONS

1. Preheat the air fryer to 180°C in the bake mode.
2. Place each chicken breast fillet between two sheets of plastic wrap. Pound them gently with a meat mallet or rolling pin until they are about 0,6 cm thick.
3. Season the chicken fillets with salt, pepper, garlic powder, and dried thyme.
4. Place 3 asparagus spears and cheese slices in the centre of each chicken fillet.
5. Roll up each chicken fillet tightly, ensuring that the filling is secure inside. Use cooking twine or toothpicks to hold the rolls together, if necessary.
6. Brush the outside of the chicken fillet rolls with olive oil.
7. Place the chicken fillet rolls in the air fryer basket seam side down.
8. Air fry for 18-20 minutes, flipping the rolls halfway through cooking, until the chicken is cooked through and golden brown.
9. Remove from the air fryer and let rest for a minute before serving.
10. Serve the air fryer chicken fillet rolls stuffed with asparagus and cheese hot, sliced if desired.

Chicken Popcorn with Dip Sauce

INSTRUCTIONS

1. Preheat the air fryer to 200°C in the bake mode.
2. Cut the chicken breasts into bite-sized pieces to form the popcorn.
3. In a shallow dish, mix together flour, breadcrumbs, paprika, garlic powder, onion powder, dried oregano, salt, and pepper to make the breading mixture.
4. Dip each chicken piece into the beaten egg, then coat it evenly with the breading mixture, pressing gently to adhere.
5. Place the coated chicken popcorn in the air fryer basket in a single layer, making sure they are not overcrowded.
6. Lightly spray the chicken popcorn with cooking spray.
7. Air fry for 10-12 minutes, shaking the basket halfway through cooking, until the chicken is crispy and golden brown.
8. While the chicken popcorn is cooking, prepare the dip sauce by mixing together mayonnaise, ketchup, honey, Dijon mustard, paprika, salt, and pepper in a small bowl.
9. Once the chicken popcorn is done, remove from the air fryer and let cool for a minute.
10. Serve the air fryer chicken popcorn hot with the dip sauce on the side for dipping.

INGREDIENTS

Ingredients for Chicken Popcorn:
* *2 boneless, skinless chicken breasts*
* *120g almond flour*
* *60g breadcrumbs*
* *1 tsp paprika*
* *1/2 tsp garlic powder*
* *1/2 tsp onion powder*
* *1/2 tsp dried oregano*
* *Salt and pepper to taste*
* *1 egg, beaten*
* *Cooking spray*

Ingredients for Dip Sauce:
* *60ml mayonnaise*
* *30ml ketchup*
* *15ml honey*
* *1 tsp Dijon mustard*
* *1/2 tsp paprika*
* *Salt and pepper to taste*

Cal 350 | Fat 15 g | Carb 25 g | Protein 25 g | Serving 2 | Cook time 25 min

MEAT RECIPES

Herb-Rubbed Pork Tenderloin

INSTRUCTIONS

1. Preheat the air fryer to 200°C in the bake mode.
2. In a small bowl, mix together olive oil, minced garlic, dried rosemary, dried thyme, dried sage, salt, and pepper to make the herb rub.
3. Pat dry the pork tenderloin with a paper towel.
4. Rub the herb mixture over the pork tenderloin, coating it evenly.
5. Lightly spray the air fryer basket with cooking spray.
6. Place the pork tenderloin in the air fryer basket.
7. Air fry for 20-25 minutes, flipping the tenderloin halfway through cooking, until it reaches an internal temperature of 63°C.
8. Remove from the air fryer and let rest for a few minutes before slicing.
9. Serve the herb-rubbed air fryer pork tenderloin hot, sliced, and enjoy!

INGREDIENTS

- *1 pork tenderloin (about 400g)*
- *30ml olive oil*
- *2 cloves garlic, minced*
- *1/2 tsp dried rosemary*
- *1/2 tsp dried thyme*
- *1/2 tsp dried sage*
- *Salt and pepper to taste*
- *Cooking spray*

Cal 250 | Fat 12 g | Carb 2 g | Protein 16 g | Serving 2 | Cook time 30 min

GARLIC LEMON LAMB CHOPS

INGREDIENTS

- 4 lamb chops
- 30ml olive oil
- 4 cloves garlic, minced
- Zest of 1 lemon
- Juice of 1 lemon
- 1/2 tsp dried oregano
- 1/2 tsp dried thyme
- Salt and pepper to taste
- Cooking spray

Cal 350 | Fat 28 g | Carb 2 g | Protein 25 g | Serving 2 | Cook time 15 min

INSTRUCTIONS

1. Preheat the air fryer to 200°C in the bake mode.
2. In a small bowl, mix together olive oil, minced garlic, lemon zest, lemon juice, dried oregano, dried thyme, salt, and pepper to make the marinade.
3. Pat dry the lamb chops with a paper towel.
4. Place the lamb chops in the marinade and toss until evenly coated. Let marinate for 15-30 minutes.
5. Lightly spray the air fryer basket with cooking spray.
6. Place the marinated lamb chops in the air fryer basket in a single layer.
7. Air fry for 8-10 minutes, flipping the chops halfway through cooking, until they reach the desired level of doneness.
8. Remove from the air fryer and let rest for a few minutes before serving.
9. Serve the garlic lemon air fryer lamb chops hot, garnished with fresh herbs if desired, and enjoy!

BBQ Spiced Beef Skewers

INSTRUCTIONS

1. Preheat the air fryer to 200°C in the bake mode.
2. In a bowl, mix together BBQ sauce, olive oil, paprika, garlic powder, onion powder, dried oregano, salt, and pepper to make the marinade.
3. Add the beef cubes to the marinade and toss until well coated. Let marinate for at least 30 minutes in the refrigerator.
4. Thread the marinated beef cubes onto the soaked wooden skewers.
5. Lightly spray the air fryer basket with cooking spray.
6. Place the beef skewers in the air fryer basket in a single layer.
7. Air fry for 10-12 minutes, flipping the skewers halfway through cooking, until the beef is cooked to your desired level of doneness and caramelized on the outside.
8. Remove from the air fryer and let rest for a minute before serving.
9. Serve the BBQ spiced air fryer beef skewers hot with your favourite sides or dipping sauce, and enjoy!

INGREDIENTS

* *300g beef sirloin, cut into cubes*
* *60ml sugar-free BBQ sauce*
* *15ml olive oil*
* *1 tsp paprika*
* *1/2 tsp garlic powder*
* *1/2 tsp onion powder*
* *1/2 tsp dried oregano*
* *Salt and pepper to taste*
* *Wooden skewers, soaked in water for 30 minutes*

Cal 300 | Fat 15 g | Carb 8 g | Protein 25 g | Serving 2 | Cook time 15 min

Cajun Seasoned Steak Strips

INGREDIENTS

- *300g beef sirloin steak, thinly sliced into strips*
- *15ml olive oil*
- *15ml Cajun seasoning*
- *1/2 tsp garlic powder*
- *1/2 tsp onion powder*
- *1/2 tsp paprika*
- *Salt and pepper to taste*

Cal 250 | Fat 15 g | Carb 2 g | Protein 25 g | Serving 2 | Cook time 15 min

INSTRUCTIONS

1. Preheat the air fryer to 200°C in the bake mode.
2. In a bowl, mix together olive oil, Cajun seasoning, garlic powder, onion powder, paprika, salt, and pepper to make the seasoning mixture.
3. Add the sliced beef sirloin strips to the seasoning mixture and toss until evenly coated.
4. Lightly spray the air fryer basket with cooking spray.
5. Place the seasoned steak strips in the air fryer basket in a single layer.
6. Air fry for 8-10 minutes, shaking the basket halfway through cooking, until the steak strips are cooked to your desired level of doneness and slightly crispy.
7. Remove from the air fryer and let rest for a minute before serving.
8. Serve the Cajun seasoned air fryer steak strips hot with your favourite sides or dipping sauce, and enjoy!

Italian Herb Air Fryer Meatballs

INSTRUCTIONS

1. Preheat the air fryer to 180°C in the bake mode.
2. In a large bowl, combine ground beef, breadcrumbs, egg, grated Parmesan cheese, minced garlic, dried basil, dried oregano, dried parsley, onion powder, salt, and pepper. Mix until well combined.
3. Shape the mixture into meatballs, about 2.5 cm in diameter.
4. Lightly spray the air fryer basket with cooking spray.
5. Place the meatballs in the air fryer basket in a single layer, leaving some space between each meatball.
6. Air fry for 12-15 minutes, shaking the basket halfway through cooking, until the meatballs are browned and cooked through.
7. Remove from the air fryer and let rest for a minute before serving.
8. Serve the Italian herb air fryer meatballs hot with your favourite pasta, sauce, or as appetizers, and enjoy!

INGREDIENTS

* *250g lean ground beef*
* *30g breadcrumbs*
* *1 egg*
* *30ml grated Parmesan cheese*
* *1 clove garlic, minced*
* *1 tsp dried basil*
* *1 tsp dried oregano*
* *1/2 tsp dried parsley*
* *1/2 tsp onion powder*
* *Salt and pepper to taste*
* *Cooking spray*

Cal 300 | Fat 15 g | Carb 8 g | Protein 25 g | Serving 2 | Cook time 20 min

HONEY MUSTARD GLAZED PORK CHOPS

INGREDIENTS

- *2 pork chops*
- *30g honey*
- *30g Dijon mustard*
- *15ml olive oil*
- *1 clove garlic, minced*
- *1/2 tsp paprika*
- *Salt and pepper to taste*

Cal 300 | Fat 15 g | Carb 15 g | Protein 25 g | Serving 2 | Cook time 20 min

INSTRUCTIONS

1. Preheat the air fryer to 200°C in the bake mode.
2. In a small bowl, whisk together honey, Dijon mustard, olive oil, minced garlic, paprika, salt, and pepper to make the glaze.
3. Pat dry the pork chops with a paper towel.
4. Brush the glaze over both sides of the pork chops, coating them evenly.
5. Lightly spray the air fryer basket with cooking spray.
6. Place the glazed pork chops in the air fryer basket in a single layer.
7. Air fry for 12-15 minutes, flipping the chops halfway through cooking, until they are cooked through and caramelized on the outside.
8. Remove from the air fryer and let rest for a minute before serving.
9. Serve the honey mustard glazed air fryer pork chops hot with your favourite sides, and enjoy!

Paprika Crusted Beef Sirloin

INSTRUCTIONS

1. Preheat the air fryer to 200°C in the bake mode.
2. In a small bowl, mix together olive oil, paprika, garlic powder, onion powder, dried thyme, salt, and pepper to make the seasoning mixture.
3. Pat dry the beef sirloin steaks with a paper towel.
4. Rub the seasoning mixture over both sides of the steaks, coating them evenly.
5. Lightly spray the air fryer basket with cooking spray.
6. Place the seasoned beef sirloin steaks in the air fryer basket in a single layer.
7. Air fry for 10-12 minutes for medium-rare, flipping the steaks halfway through cooking, or adjust the time based on your desired level of doneness.
8. Remove from the air fryer and let rest for a minute before serving.
9. Serve the paprika crusted air fryer beef sirloin hot with your favourite sides or sauces, and enjoy!

INGREDIENTS

- *2 beef sirloin steaks (about 200g each)*
- *30ml olive oil*
- *2 tsp paprika*
- *1/2 tsp garlic powder*
- *1/2 tsp onion powder*
- *1/2 tsp dried thyme*
- *Salt and pepper to taste*

Cal 350 | Fat 20 g | Carb 2 g | Protein 16 g | Serving 2 | Cook time 20 min

MEDITERRANEAN SPICE LAMB KEBABS

INGREDIENTS

- *300g lamb leg meat, cubed*
- *15ml olive oil*
- *1/2 tsp paprika*
- *1/2 tsp ground cumin*
- *1/2 tsp dried oregano*
- *1/2 tsp garlic powder*
- *1/2 tsp onion powder*
- *Salt and pepper to taste*
- *Wooden skewers, soaked in water for 30 minutes*

Cal 300 | Fat 20 g | Carb 2 g | Protein 25 g | Serving 2 | Cook time 25 min

INSTRUCTIONS

1. Preheat the air fryer to 200°C in the bake mode.
2. In a bowl, combine olive oil, paprika, ground cumin, dried oregano, garlic powder, onion powder, salt, and pepper to make the marinade.
3. Add the cubed lamb meat to the marinade and toss until well coated. Let marinate for at least 30 minutes in the refrigerator.
4. Thread the marinated lamb cubes onto the soaked wooden skewers.
5. Lightly spray the air fryer basket with cooking spray.
6. Place the lamb kebabs in the air fryer basket in a single layer.
7. Air fry for 10-12 minutes, flipping the kebabs halfway through cooking, until the lamb is cooked to your desired level of doneness.
8. Remove from the air fryer and let rest for a minute before serving.
9. Serve the Mediterranean spice air fryer lamb kebabs hot with your favourite sides or dipping sauce, and enjoy!

Greek-style Lamb Souvlaki

INSTRUCTIONS

1. Preheat the air fryer to 200°C in the bake mode.
2. In a bowl, combine olive oil, minced garlic, lemon juice, dried oregano, dried thyme, salt, and pepper to make the marinade.
3. Add the cubed lamb meat to the marinade and toss until well coated. Let marinate for at least 30 minutes in the refrigerator.
4. Thread the marinated lamb cubes onto the soaked wooden skewers.
5. Lightly spray the air fryer basket with cooking spray.
6. Place the lamb souvlaki skewers in the air fryer basket in a single layer.
7. Air fry for 10-12 minutes, flipping the skewers halfway through cooking, until the lamb is cooked to your desired level of doneness and slightly charred on the outside.
8. Remove from the air fryer and let rest for a minute before serving.
9. Serve the Greek-style air fryer lamb souvlaki hot with pita bread, tzatziki sauce, and your favourite Greek salad, and enjoy!

INGREDIENTS

- 300g lamb leg meat, cubed
- 30ml olive oil
- 2 cloves garlic, minced
- Juice of 1 lemon
- 1/2 tsp dried oregano
- 1/2 tsp dried thyme
- Salt and pepper to taste
- Wooden skewers, soaked in water for 30 minutes

Cal 350 | Fat 25 g | Carb 2 g | Protein 25 g | Serving 2 | Cook time 20 min

BBQ Beef Ribs

INGREDIENTS

- *500g beef ribs*
- *120ml sugar-free BBQ sauce*
- *15ml olive oil*
- *1 tsp paprika*
- *1/2 tsp garlic powder*
- *1/2 tsp onion powder*
- *Salt and pepper to taste*

Cal 350 | Fat 25 g | Carb 2 g | Protein 25 g | Serving 2 | Cook time 20 min

INSTRUCTIONS

1. Preheat the air fryer to 180°C in the bake mode.
2. In a bowl, mix together BBQ sauce, olive oil, paprika, garlic powder, onion powder, salt, and pepper.
3. Brush the BBQ sauce mixture over the beef ribs, coating them evenly.
4. Place the beef ribs in the air fryer basket, making sure they are not overcrowded.
5. Air fry for 25-30 minutes, flipping the ribs halfway through cooking, until they are tender and cooked through.
6. Remove from the air fryer and let rest for a few minutes before serving.
7. Serve the air fryer BBQ beef ribs hot with your favourite side dishes and enjoy!

VEGETABLE RECIPES

STUFFED SWEET PEPPERS

INGREDIENTS

* *2 sweet peppers (any colour), halved and seeds removed*
* *200g cooked quinoa*
* *100g cherry tomatoes, halved*
* *60g crumbled feta cheese*
* *2 tbsp chopped Kalamata olives*
* *1 tsp chopped fresh parsley*
* *1 tsp chopped fresh basil*
* *1 clove garlic, minced*
* *15ml olive oil*
* *Salt and pepper to taste*
* *Cooking spray*

Cal 200 | Fat 9 g | Carb 25 g | Protein 6 g | Serving 2 | Cook time 20 min

INSTRUCTIONS

1. Preheat the air fryer to 180°C in the bake mode.
2. In a mixing bowl, combine cooked quinoa, cherry tomatoes, feta cheese, Kalamata olives, parsley, basil, minced garlic, olive oil, salt, and pepper. Mix well.
3. Spoon the quinoa mixture into each Sweet Pepper half, filling them evenly.
4. Lightly spray the air fryer basket with cooking spray.
5. Place the stuffed sweet peppers in the air fryer basket, cut side up.
6. Air fry for 12-15 minutes, until the peppers are tender and the filling is heated through.
7. Remove from the air fryer and let cool for a few minutes before serving.
8. Serve the Mediterranean stuffed air fryer sweet peppers hot as a delicious and nutritious meal.

Lemon Herb Air Fryer Asparagus Spears

INSTRUCTIONS

1. Preheat the air fryer to 200°C in the bake mode.
2. In a small bowl, whisk together olive oil, lemon zest, lemon juice, dried thyme, dried rosemary, garlic powder, salt, and pepper to make the marinade.
3. Place the trimmed asparagus spears in a shallow dish and pour the marinade over them. Toss to coat evenly.
4. Lightly spray the air fryer basket with cooking spray.
5. Place the marinated asparagus spears in the air fryer basket in a single layer.
6. Air fry for 8-10 minutes, shaking the basket halfway through cooking, until the asparagus is tender and slightly charred.
7. Remove from the air fryer and serve the lemon herb air fryer asparagus spears hot as a delightful side dish.

INGREDIENTS

* *1 bunch asparagus spears, trimmed*
* *30ml olive oil*
* *Zest of 1 lemon*
* *Juice of 1 lemon*
* *1/2 tsp dried thyme*
* *1/2 tsp dried rosemary*
* *1/2 tsp garlic powder*
* *Salt and pepper to taste*
* *Cooking spray*

Cal 80 | Fat 7 g | Carb 5 g | Protein 3 g | Serving 2 | Cook time 12 min

SESAME GINGER BROCCOLI FLORETS

INGREDIENTS

- *1 head broccoli, cut into florets*
- *30ml sesame oil*
- *15ml soy sauce*
- *15ml rice vinegar*
- *15g honey*
- *1/2 tsp grated ginger*
- *1/2 tsp sesame seeds*
- *Salt and pepper to taste*

Cal 80 | Fat 5 g | Carb 9 g | Protein 3 g | Serving 2 | Cook time 15 min

INSTRUCTIONS

1. Preheat the air fryer to 180°C in the bake mode.
2. In a small bowl, whisk together sesame oil, soy sauce, rice vinegar, honey, grated ginger, sesame seeds, salt, and pepper to make the marinade.
3. Place the broccoli florets in a mixing bowl and pour the marinade over them. Toss to coat evenly.
4. Lightly spray the air fryer basket with cooking spray.
5. Place the marinated broccoli florets in the air fryer basket in a single layer.
6. Air fry for 10-12 minutes, shaking the basket halfway through cooking, until the broccoli is tender and slightly crispy.
7. Remove from the air fryer and serve the sesame ginger air fryer broccoli florets hot as a nutritious side dish or snack.

AIR FRYER RATATOUILLE

INSTRUCTIONS

1. Preheat the air fryer to 180°C in the bake mode.
2. In a large bowl, combine diced aubergine, courgette, yellow squash, sweet pepper, onion, garlic, and tomatoes.
3. Drizzle olive oil over the vegetables and sprinkle with dried thyme, dried oregano, dried basil, salt, and pepper. Toss until the vegetables are evenly coated.
4. Lightly spray the air fryer basket with cooking spray.
5. Transfer the seasoned vegetables to the air fryer basket, spreading them out in a single layer.
6. Air fry for 15-20 minutes, shaking the basket halfway through cooking, until the vegetables are tender and slightly caramelized.
7. Remove from the air fryer and let cool for a few minutes before serving.
8. Serve the air fryer ratatouille hot as a delightful and nutritious side dish.

INGREDIENTS

- *1 medium aubergine, diced*
- *1 medium courgette, diced*
- *1 medium yellow squash, diced*
- *1 sweet pepper, diced*
- *1 onion, diced*
- *2 cloves garlic, minced*
- *2 tomatoes, diced*
- *30ml olive oil*
- *1/2 tsp dried thyme*
- *1/2 tsp dried oregano*
- *1/2 tsp dried basil*
- *Salt and pepper to taste*

Cal 120 | Fat 6 g | Carb 16 g | Protein 3 g | Serving 2 | Cook time 20 min

BEETROOT WITH ORANGE GREMOLATA AND GOAT CHEESE

INSTRUCTIONS

1. Preheat the air fryer to 180°C in the bake mode.
2. In a bowl, toss the beet wedges with olive oil, salt, and pepper until evenly coated.
3. Place the seasoned beet wedges in the air fryer basket in a single layer.
4. Air fry for 15-20 minutes, shaking the basket halfway through cooking, until the beetroot are tender and slightly caramelized.
5. Meanwhile, prepare the orange gremolata by combining chopped parsley, orange zest, and minced garlic in a small bowl.
6. Once the beetroot are cooked, transfer them to a serving dish and sprinkle with crumbled goat cheese.
7. Top the beetroot with the prepared orange gremolata.
8. Serve the air-fryer beetroot with orange gremolata and goat cheese as a vibrant and flavorful side dish.

INGREDIENTS

* 450g medium beetroot, peeled and sliced into wedges
* 30ml olive oil
* Salt and pepper to taste
* 60g fresh parsley, finely chopped
* Zest of 1 orange
* 1 clove garlic, minced
* 30g crumbled goat cheese

Cal 120 | Fat 8 g | Carb 8 g | Protein 3 g | Serving 2 | Cook time 25 min

Fried Avocado Tacos

INSTRUCTIONS

1. Preheat the air fryer to 200°C in the bake mode.
2. In a shallow dish, mix breadcrumbs, grated Parmesan cheese, chili powder, garlic powder, paprika, salt, and pepper to create the breading mixture.
3. Dip avocado slices into the beaten egg, then coat them evenly with the breadcrumb mixture.
4. Lightly spray the air fryer basket with cooking spray.
5. Place the breaded avocado slices in the air fryer basket in a single layer, making sure they are not touching.
6. Air fry for 5-7 minutes, flipping halfway through cooking, until the avocado slices are golden and crispy.
7. While the avocado slices are cooking, warm the corn tortillas in a dry skillet or microwave.
8. Assemble the tacos by placing fried avocado slices in warmed tortillas and topping with shredded lettuce, diced tomatoes, sliced jalapeños, salsa, sour cream, and a squeeze of lime juice.
9. Serve the air-fryer fried avocado tacos immediately and enjoy!

INGREDIENTS

- *2 ripe avocados, sliced*
- *60g gluten-free breadcrumbs*
- *25g grated Parmesan cheese*
- *1 tsp chili powder*
- *1/2 tsp garlic powder*
- *1/2 tsp paprika*
- *Salt and pepper to taste*
- *1 egg, beaten*
- *Cooking spray*
- *6 small corn tortillas*
- *Toppings (optional): shredded lettuce, diced tomatoes, sliced jalapeños, salsa, sour cream, lime wedges*

Cal 250 | Fat 12 g | Carb 26 g | Protein 6 g | Serving 2 | Cook time 10 min

PORTOBELLO MELTS

INSTRUCTIONS

1. Preheat the air fryer to 180°C in the bake mode.
2. In a small bowl, whisk together balsamic vinegar, olive oil, minced garlic, salt, and pepper.
3. Brush both sides of the portobello mushrooms with the balsamic vinegar mixture.
4. Place the mushrooms in the air fryer basket, gill side up.
5. Air fry for 5 minutes.
6. Flip the mushrooms and sprinkle shredded mozzarella cheese and grated Parmesan cheese evenly over the gill side of each mushroom.
7. Top each mushroom with a slice of tomato and a few fresh basil leaves.
8. Air fry for an additional 5 minutes, or until the cheese is melted and bubbly.
9. Remove from the air fryer and serve the portobello melts hot as a delicious appetizer or light meal.

INGREDIENTS

* 2 large portobello mushrooms, stems removed
* 30ml balsamic vinegar
* 30ml olive oil
* 2 cloves garlic, minced
* Salt and pepper to taste
* 50g shredded mozzarella cheese
* 25g grated Parmesan cheese
* 2 slices tomato
* Fresh basil leaves
* Cooking spray

Cal 180 | Fat 12 g | Carb 8 g | Protein 16 g | Serving 2 | Cook time 15 min

CHICKPEA FRITTERS

INSTRUCTIONS

1. Preheat the air fryer to 200°C in the bake mode.
2. In a food processor, combine half of the chickpeas, chopped onion, minced garlic, fresh parsley, ground cumin, ground coriander, paprika, salt, and pepper. Pulse until the mixture is well combined but still slightly chunky.
3. Transfer the chickpea mixture to a mixing bowl and stir in chickpea flour until the mixture holds together.
4. Divide the mixture into 4 equal portions and shape each portion into a small patty.
5. Lightly spray the air fryer basket with cooking spray.
6. Place the chickpea fritters in the air fryer basket in a single layer, leaving space between each fritter.
7. Air fry for 10-12 minutes, flipping halfway through cooking, until the fritters are golden brown and crispy.
8. Remove from the air fryer and let cool for a few minutes before serving.
9. Serve the air-fryer chickpea fritters hot as a nutritious snack or appetizer, or as part of a meal.

INGREDIENTS

- *1/2 can (200g) chickpeas, drained and rinsed*
- *1/2 small onion, finely chopped*
- *1 clove garlic, minced*
- *1 tbsp chopped fresh parsley*
- *1/2 tsp ground cumin*
- *1/4 tsp ground coriander*
- *1/8 tsp paprika*
- *Salt and pepper to taste*
- *1 tbsp chickpea flour (or all-purpose flour)*
- *Cooking spray*

Cal 120 | Fat 2 g | Carb 20 g | Protein 6 g | Serving 2 | Cook time 15 min

SWEET PEPPER STUFFED WITH MUSHROOMS AND CHEESE

INGREDIENTS

- *2 large sweet peppers, halved and seeds removed*
- *200g mushrooms, diced*
- *1 small onion, finely chopped*
- *2 cloves garlic, minced*
- *1 tbsp olive oil*
- *1/2 tsp dried thyme*
- *1/2 tsp dried oregano*
- *Salt and pepper to taste*
- *100g mozzarella cheese, shredded*
- *Fresh parsley, chopped (for garnish)*

Cal 180 | Fat 9 g | Carb 15 g | Protein 8 g | Serving 2 | Cook time 20 min

INSTRUCTIONS

1. Preheat the air fryer to 180°C in the bake mode.
2. In a skillet, heat olive oil over medium heat. Add chopped onion and minced garlic, and sauté until translucent.
3. Add diced mushrooms to the skillet and cook until they release their moisture and become tender.
4. Season the mushroom mixture with dried thyme, dried oregano, salt, and pepper. Stir well to combine.
5. Arrange the sweet pepper halves in the air fryer basket.
6. Spoon the cooked mushroom mixture into each sweet pepper half, filling them evenly.
7. Sprinkle shredded mozzarella cheese over the stuffed sweet peppers.
8. Air fry for 12-15 minutes, or until the sweet peppers are tender and the cheese is melted and bubbly.
9. Remove from the air fryer and let cool for a few minutes.
10. Garnish with chopped fresh parsley before serving.
11. Serve the air-fryer sweet peppers stuffed with mushrooms and mozzarella cheese hot as a delicious and nutritious meal.

Vegan Courgette Lasagna

INSTRUCTIONS

1. Preheat the air fryer to 180°C in the bake mode.
2. In a skillet, heat olive oil over medium heat. Add diced onion and minced garlic, and sauté until translucent.
3. Add sliced mushrooms to the skillet and cook until they release their moisture and become tender.
4. Stir in diced tomatoes, dried oregano, dried basil, salt, and pepper. Cook for another 2-3 minutes, then remove from heat.
5. In a small bowl, mix together vegan ricotta cheese and spinach leaves.
6. Lightly spray the air fryer basket with cooking spray.
7. Arrange a layer of sliced courgette in the bottom of the air fryer basket.
8. Spread a layer of marinara sauce over the courgette slices.
9. Top with a layer of the vegan ricotta cheese and spinach mixture, followed by a layer of the mushroom and tomato mixture.
10. Repeat the layers until all ingredients are used, finishing with a layer of marinara sauce on top.
11. If desired, sprinkle vegan mozzarella cheese on top of the lasagna.
12. Air fry for 20-25 minutes, or until the courgette is tender and the lasagna is heated through.
13. Remove from the air fryer and let cool for a few minutes before serving.
14. Garnish with fresh basil leaves before serving.
15. Serve the air-fryer vegan courgette lasagna hot as a hearty and flavorful meal.

INGREDIENTS

* *2 large courgettes, thinly sliced lengthwise*
* *240 ml marinara sauce*
* *240g vegan ricotta cheese*
* *40g spinach leaves*
* *120g diced tomatoes*
* *60g sliced mushrooms*
* *60g diced onion*
* *2 cloves garlic, minced*
* *15ml olive oil*
* *1/2 tsp dried oregano*
* *1/2 tsp dried basil*
* *Salt and pepper to taste*
* *Vegan mozzarella cheese (optional)*
* *Fresh basil leaves for garnish*

Cal 180 | Fat 9 g | Carb 15 g | Protein 8 g | Serving 2 | Cook time 30 min

DESSERTS

Chocolate Donuts

INSTRUCTIONS

1. In a mixing bowl, combine almond flour, cocoa powder, powdered erythritol, lemon zest, lemon juice, vanilla extract, baking powder, and a pinch of salt.
2. Add unsweetened applesauce and vegetable oil to the dry ingredients and mix until well combined.
3. Beat the egg separately and then add it to the mixture, stirring until a smooth batter forms.
4. Preheat the air fryer to 180°C in the bake mode.
5. Lightly grease the cavities of a donut pan with cooking spray.
6. Spoon the batter into the prepared donut pan, filling each cavity about two-thirds full.
7. Place the filled donut pan in the preheated air fryer and bake for 8-10 minutes, or until the donuts are firm to the touch and a toothpick inserted into the centre comes out clean.
8. Once baked, remove the donuts from the air fryer and let them cool in the pan for a few minutes before transferring them to a wire rack to cool completely.
9. Serve the air-fryer chocolate donuts once cooled, and enjoy!

INGREDIENTS

* *100g almond flour*
* *25g cocoa powder (unsweetened)*
* *25g powdered erythritol (or another sugar substitute)*
* *Zest of 1/2 lemon*
* *1 tbsp fresh lemon juice*
* *1/2 tsp vanilla extract*
* *1/4 tsp baking powder*
* *Pinch of salt*
* *1 tbsp unsweetened applesauce*
* *1 tbsp vegetable oil*
* *1 large egg*

Cal 70 | Fat 6 g | Carb 2 g | Protein 3 g | Serving 2 | Cook time 20 min

LEMON COOKIES

INGREDIENTS

- *100g almond flour*
- *25g coconut flour*
- *25g powdered erythritol (or another sugar substitute)*
- *Zest of 1 lemon*
- *2 tbsp fresh lemon juice*
- *1/2 tsp vanilla extract*
- *1/4 tsp baking powder*
- *Pinch of salt*
- *2 tbsp unsalted butter, softened*
- *1 large egg*

Cal 100 | Fat 8 g | Carb 4 g | Protein 3 g | Serving 2 | Cook time 15 min

INSTRUCTIONS

1. In a mixing bowl, combine almond flour, coconut flour, powdered erythritol, lemon zest, lemon juice, vanilla extract, baking powder, and a pinch of salt.
2. Add softened butter to the dry ingredients and mix until well combined and crumbly.
3. Add the egg and continue to mix until a dough forms. If the dough is too dry, add a teaspoon of water at a time until it comes together.
4. Shape the dough into a log, about 3.8cm in diameter, and wrap it tightly in parchment paper or plastic wrap.
5. Place the wrapped dough in the refrigerator and chill for at least 30 minutes, or until firm.
6. Preheat the air fryer to 160°C in the bake mode.
7. Once chilled, unwrap the dough and slice it into 0.6cm thick rounds.
8. Place the cookie rounds on a parchment-lined air fryer basket or tray, leaving space between each cookie.
9. Air fry the cookies for 8-10 minutes, or until the edges are golden brown.
10. Remove the cookies from the air fryer and let them cool on a wire rack.
11. Once cooled, store the cookies in an airtight container at room temperature.

Chocolate Cake

INSTRUCTIONS

1. Preheat the air fryer to 160°C in the bake mode.
2. In a mixing bowl, combine almond flour, cocoa powder, powdered erythritol, baking powder, and a pinch of salt.
3. In another bowl, whisk together eggs, almond milk, melted coconut oil, and vanilla extract until well combined.
4. Pour the wet ingredients into the dry ingredients and mix until smooth.
5. Lightly grease a small cake pan that fits inside your air fryer with cooking spray.
6. Pour the batter into the prepared cake pan and spread it evenly.
7. Place the cake pan in the preheated air fryer basket.
8. Air fry the cake for 20-25 minutes, or until a toothpick inserted into the centre comes out clean.
9. Once done, remove the cake from the air fryer and let it cool in the pan for a few minutes.
10. Transfer the cake to a wire rack to cool completely before slicing and serving.
11. Serve the air fryer chocolate cake plain or with whipped cream or berries, if desired.

INGREDIENTS

* *90g almond flour*
* *25g unsweetened cocoa powder*
* *25g powdered erythritol (or another sugar substitute)*
* *1/2 tsp baking powder*
* *Pinch of salt*
* *2 medium eggs*
* *60ml unsweetened almond milk*
* *15ml melted coconut oil*
* *2.5ml vanilla extract*

Cal 315 | Fat 26 g | Carb 12 g | Protein 11 g | Serving 2 | Cook time 35 min

BAKED PEARS WITH ALMOND CRUMBLE

INGREDIENTS

- *2 ripe pears*
- *20g almond flour*
- *20g rolled oats*
- *10g chopped almonds*
- *10g unsalted butter, melted*
- *10g powdered erythritol (or another sugar substitute)*
- *5ml lemon juice*
- *1/4 tsp ground cinnamon*
- *Pinch of salt*

Cal 150 | Fat 8 g | Carb 17 g | Protein 3 g | Serving 2 | Cook time 20 min

INSTRUCTIONS

1. Preheat the air fryer to 180°C in the bake mode.
2. Cut the pears in half lengthwise and remove the cores with a spoon, creating a hollow in the centre of each pear half.
3. Place the pear halves, cut side up, in the air fryer basket or on a baking sheet lined with parchment paper.
4. In a mixing bowl, combine almond flour, rolled oats, chopped almonds, melted butter, powdered erythritol, lemon juice, ground cinnamon, and a pinch of salt. Mix until crumbly.
5. Fill each pear half with the almond crumble mixture, pressing it gently onto the surface of the pears.
6. Place the filled pear halves in the preheated air fryer.
7. Air fry the pears for 12-15 minutes, or until the pears are tender and the almond crumble is golden brown and crispy.
8. Remove the baked pears from the air fryer and let them cool for a few minutes before serving.
9. Serve the air-fryer baked pears warm, optionally with a drizzle of honey or a scoop of vanilla ice cream.

BANANA CHIPS WITH CINNAMON

INSTRUCTIONS

1. Preheat the air fryer to 160°C in the bake mode.
2. Peel the bananas and slice them into thin rounds, about 3mm thick.
3. Place the banana slices in a bowl and toss them with lemon juice to prevent browning.
4. Arrange the banana slices in a single layer in the air fryer basket or on a baking sheet lined with parchment paper.
5. Sprinkle the banana slices with ground cinnamon.
6. Air fry the banana slices for 10-12 minutes, flipping them halfway through, until they are crisp and golden brown.
7. Once done, remove the banana chips from the air fryer and let them cool completely before serving.
8. Serve the air-fryer banana chips as a healthy snack or a crunchy topping for yogurt or oatmeal.

INGREDIENTS

* *2 ripe bananas*
* *5ml lemon juice*
* *1/2 tsp ground cinnamon*

Cal 70 | Fat 0 g | Carb 18 g | Protein 1 g | Serving 2 | Cook time 20 min

PEACH COBBLER WITH OAT CRUMBLE

INGREDIENTS

- *2 ripe peaches, peeled, pitted, and sliced*
- *10g lemon juice*
- *10g powdered erythritol (or another sugar substitute)*
- *1 tsp cornstarch*
- *30g rolled oats*
- *20g almond flour*
- *15g unsalted butter, melted*
- *10g chopped pecans*
- *5g powdered erythritol (for crumble)*
- *1/4 tsp ground cinnamon*
- *Pinch of salt*

Cal 160 | Fat 9 g | Carb 15 g | Protein 3 g | Serving 2 | Cook time 20 min

INSTRUCTIONS

1. Preheat the air fryer to 180°C in the bake mode.
2. In a bowl, combine the sliced peaches with lemon juice, powdered erythritol, and cornstarch. Toss until the peaches are coated evenly.
3. In another bowl, mix together the rolled oats, almond flour, melted butter, chopped pecans, powdered erythritol (for crumble), ground cinnamon, and a pinch of salt until crumbly.
4. Divide the peach mixture evenly between two ramekins or oven-safe dishes.
5. Sprinkle the oat crumble mixture over the top of the peaches in each ramekin.
6. Place the ramekins in the preheated air fryer basket.
7. Air fry the peach cobblers for 12-15 minutes, or until the topping is golden brown and the peaches are bubbly.
8. Remove the ramekins from the air fryer and let them cool for a few minutes before serving.
9. Serve the air-fryer peach cobblers warm, optionally with a scoop of vanilla ice cream or whipped cream.

Vanilla Bean Air Fryer Custard Cups

INSTRUCTIONS

1. Preheat the air fryer to 160°C in the bake mode.
2. In a mixing bowl, whisk together the eggs, almond milk, powdered erythritol, vanilla extract, and scraped vanilla bean seeds until well combined.
3. Pour the custard mixture into two small ramekins or oven-safe dishes.
4. Place the ramekins in the preheated air fryer basket.
5. Air fry the custard cups for 15-20 minutes, or until the custard is set around the edges but still slightly jiggly in the centre.
6. Once done, remove the custard cups from the air fryer and let them cool to room temperature.
7. Refrigerate the custard cups for at least 1 hour before serving.
8. Serve the vanilla bean air-fryer custard cups chilled, optionally with a sprinkle of ground cinnamon or fresh berries on top.

INGREDIENTS

* *2 large eggs*
* *200ml unsweetened almond milk*
* *20g powdered erythritol (or another sugar substitute)*
* *5ml vanilla extract*
* *1 vanilla bean pod, seeds scraped out (optional)*

Cal 70 | Fat 4 g | Carb 2 g | Protein 5 g | Serving 2 | Cook time 20 min

COCONUT MACAROONS

INGREDIENTS

- *100g shredded coconut*
- *50g powdered erythritol (or another sugar substitute)*
- *2 large egg whites*
- *5ml vanilla extract*
- *Pinch of salt*

Cal 80 | Fat 7 g | Carb 3 g | Protein 1 g | Serving 2 | Cook time 20 min

INSTRUCTIONS

1. Preheat the air fryer to 160°C in the bake mode.
2. In a mixing bowl, combine the shredded coconut and powdered erythritol.
3. In another bowl, whisk the egg whites until they form stiff peaks.
4. Gently fold the egg whites into the coconut mixture until well combined.
5. Add the vanilla extract and a pinch of salt, and mix until incorporated.
6. Using a spoon or a cookie scoop, shape the coconut mixture into small mounds and place them on a parchment-lined air fryer basket.
7. Air fry the coconut macaroons for 10-12 minutes, or until they are lightly golden brown on the outside.
8. Once done, remove the coconut macaroons from the air fryer and let them cool completely before serving.
9. Serve the air-fryer coconut macaroons as a delicious and guilt-free dessert option.

Lemon-Blueberry Muffins

INSTRUCTIONS

1. Preheat your air fryer to 180°C.
2. In a mixing bowl, combine the almond flour, granulated sweetener, lemon zest, baking powder, baking soda, and a pinch of salt.
3. In a separate bowl, whisk together the vegetable oil, almond milk, lemon juice, and egg.
4. Gradually add the wet ingredients to the dry ingredients, stirring until just combined.
5. Gently fold in the fresh blueberries.
6. Divide the batter evenly among 6 muffin cups lined with paper liners or sprayed with cooking spray.
7. Place the muffin cups in the air fryer basket, ensuring they are not overcrowded.
8. Air fry the muffins at 180°C for about 12-15 minutes, or until they are golden brown and a toothpick inserted into the centre comes out clean.

INGREDIENTS

* *150g almond flour*
* *75g granulated sweetener suitable for baking (e.g., erythritol or stevia)*
* *Zest of 1 lemon*
* *Juice of 1/2 lemon*
* *1 tsp baking powder*
* *1/4 tsp baking soda*
* *Pinch of salt*
* *60ml vegetable oil*
* *120ml unsweetened almond milk (or any milk of your choice)*
* *1 large egg*
* *100g fresh blueberries*

Cal 80 | Fat 7 g | Carb 3 g | Protein 1 g | Serving 2 | Cook time 20 min

CHEESECAKE CHIMICHANGAS

INGREDIENTS

- *200g reduced-fat cream cheese, softened*
- *30g granulated sweetener suitable for baking (e.g., erythritol or stevia)*
- *1 tsp vanilla extract*
- *4 small almond flour tortillas*
- *2 tbsp unsalted butter, melted*
- *1/2 tsp ground cinnamon*
- *Cooking spray*
- *Fresh berries for serving (optional)*
- *Greek yogurt or sugar-free whipped cream for serving (optional)*

Cal 80 | Fat 7 g | Carb 3 g | Protein 1 g | Serving 2 | Cook time 20 min

INSTRUCTIONS

1. In a mixing bowl, beat the softened cream cheese, granulated sweetener, and vanilla extract until smooth and well combined.
2. Lay out the almond flour tortillas and divide the cream cheese mixture evenly among them, spreading it down the centre of each tortilla.
3. Fold the sides of each tortilla over the filling, then roll up tightly to form chimichangas.
4. In a small bowl, mix the melted unsalted butter with the ground cinnamon.
5. Lightly spray the chimichangas with cooking spray to help them crisp up in the air fryer.
6. Preheat your air fryer to 180°C.
7. Place the chimichangas seam side down in the air fryer basket, ensuring they are not overcrowded.
8. Air fry the chimichangas for 8-10 minutes or until they are golden brown and crispy.
9. Remove the chimichangas from the air fryer and brush them with the cinnamon butter mixture.
10. Serve the chimichangas warm, optionally topped with fresh berries and a dollop of Greek yogurt or sugar-free whipped cream.

CONCLUSION

As you embark on your culinary journey through the Diabetic Air Fryer Cookbook, remember that delicious, satisfying meals are not only possible but also beneficial for managing diabetes. By harnessing the power of the air fryer and focusing on whole, nutrient-dense ingredients, you can create meals that not only help regulate blood sugar levels but also promote overall health and well-being.

Whether you're craving hearty main courses, or indulgent desserts, you'll find a wealth of flavorful options to enjoy guilt-free. Each recipe has been meticulously crafted to adhere to the dietary requirements of those with diabetes while never compromising on taste or satisfaction.

As you explore the recipes within these pages, may you find inspiration and empowerment to take control of your health through the joy of cooking. With the Diabetic Air Fryer Cookbook as your guide, delicious, diabetes-friendly meals are just a recipe away. Here's to happy, healthy eating and a lifetime of culinary adventures!

Printed in Great Britain
by Amazon

49541417R00056